THE GUIDE TO

HAWAIIAN STYLE

ORIGAMI

by

Jodi Fukumoto

ISLAND HERITAGE

Table of Contents

Introduction • 4

Dedication & Acknowledgements • 6

Basic Supplies • 7

Learn Origami
Please Read • 7
The Fundamentals • 7
Steps and Drawings • 9
Lines, Arrows & Simple Folds • 10
Combination Folds • 15

The Models *(In Order of Difficulty)*

The Aloha Shirt • 22

The Volcano - *Crater and Eruption* • 28

The Humuhumunukunukuāpuaʻa - *State Fish* • 36

The Anthurium • 46

The Hibiscus - *State Flower* • 58

The Plumeria • 66

The Marlin • 72

The Gecko • 84

The Snow King Protea • 96

The Orchid • 106

The Hula Dancer • 122

The Double Hull Canoe • 134

The Bird of Paradise • 146

The Torch Ginger • 160

From a Sea of Paper - *A Supplement on Paper*

Origami Paper • 172

Cutting the Perfect Square • 172

Selecting Paper • 174

Printed Paper • 174

Layering • 174

Wet Folding • 179

Paper Description of Models • 180

Introduction

In this, her first book, Jodi Fukumoto applies the ancient art of origami ("oru" - to fold, "kami" - paper), to an array of Hawaiian shapes and symbols, creating three-dimensional objects of spectacular beauty.

From volcanoes to voyaging canoes, each is an original expression of true Hawaiiana: tropical flowers and fish, aloha shirts, a hula dancer... even a whimsical gecko. Designs for those new to the art form and more detailed models for the experienced folder are included. All will benefit from Jodi's expressive style, attention to detail, and clear, easy-to-follow instructions.

In the special section, A *Sea of Paper*, the author offers in-depth definitions, descriptions, and methodology. In *Layering,* she explains her innovative style of combining paper and textiles for dramatic effects in color and dimension. The hands-on format will inspire you to share in Jodi's tremendous talent as you spend hours of enjoyment folding your own beautiful origami ornaments.

Throughout our long friendship, I've observed Jodi's constant focus on following her innate artistic desires, including her passionate dream to write and design this book. She was always folding, refolding, and refiguring. Experimentation followed determination. Series emerged; shapes and forms inspired each other. Then, in 1995, her daughter Kiara was born, adding a whole new level of joy and inspiration, further stretching her intuition and imagination.

Jodi's models were first viewed in public in 1997 at the Hawaii State Library in Honolulu, then at the Kamehameha School libraries. During one showing, a reporter recommended her vibrant artwork to a television newsman who sought her out for a live interview. I recall the morning's excitement! This exposure heightened Jodi's enthusiasm, and public interest in her Hawaiian originals continued to grow.

In 1998, the Bishop Museum selected Jodi as a crafter/demonstrator in their Hawaiian Hall—an incredible honor as it marked the first time Jodi's work was recognized as an expression of Hawaiiana. At the same time, she was featured on the popular local program, "The Hawaiian Moving Company," and soon after she appeared at the Japanese Cultural Center's festive New Year celebration. Participants were in awe of her creativity as she demonstrated her lifelike paper ornaments, and many folded their own models of a version of *The Aloha Shirt*.

In the spring of 1999, Jodi taught at Windward Community College in Kaneohe and at the Temari Center for Asian and Pacific Arts in Honolulu. Her next engagement was with the Pearl City Library's 50th Anniversary Celebration. Each interaction with the public strengthened Jodi's determination to write and illustrate a book which would combine her Japanese cultural heritage—and the art of origami—with her life in Hawaii.

What a true journey of courageous and artistic effort it is to have **Hawaiian Style Origami** in print at last. Please join me in congratulating this incredible woman for her vision, inspiration, perseverance, and creative excellence.

With tremendous appreciation and admiration,
Your friend, Margo Elbert

This book is dedicated to Kiara
Mahalo to:

My mother, Barbara Fukumoto, for everything.

Mrs. Taeko Murakami for her sincere help and involvement with
this project throughout the years.

Jan Fodor of *Origami by Jan* for her effort toward establishing me in
the origami community, for her Internet research on creating origami books,
and for sharing her work and ideas.

Preston Terada of *Ink Trails Graphics* for his qualified advice on
computer illustration.

Margo Elbert for writing the introduction with notable thought and style.
Artist Susan Cardenas for painting the beautiful tapa pattern on
The Double Hull Canoe model.

Paul Fodor for creating the cute wire hangers for *The Aloha Shirt* models.
Mr. Dean Nagamine for his valuable time and professional legal advice.
Aimee Muira for her reliable knowledge and understanding of origami.

🌸   🌸   🌸

Thanks also to my sisters, Joy Murakami and Joan Fukumoto; the owners and
staff at Koa House Restaurant; George and Elaine Oshiro; Russell Ito; and of
course, Island Heritage.

Basic Supplies

You will need *origami paper* (perfectly square sheets of paper approximately 6 and 10-inches square or larger in assorted colors) to fold the models in this book. For more information, refer to *Origami Paper* in the supplement, *From a Sea of Paper*.

Learn Origami

Please Read

To the experienced folder: This section is written with consideration for the beginner, however it does contain a few terms and folds used exclusively in this book. Please review *Lines, Arrows & Simple Folds* and *Combination Folds*.

To the beginner: Please start by reading *The Fundamentals*, which explains the origami instruction and offers tips on folding. Become familiar with *Lines, Arrows & Simple Folds*, your key to folding. It is not necessary to memorize all the different arrows and simple folds. You will learn as you fold, for each applied arrow and simple fold is described in either the model instructions or in the guide, *Combination Folds*. Please learn the six kinds of lines and two symbols. It is also helpful to understand the *mountain fold (mtn. fold)*.

Review the guide, *Combination Folds*. Realize that each combination fold is nothing more than combined simple folds. In fact, only two new instructional arrows are introduced outside the key. Combination folds are best learned through application.

The models appear in order of difficulty. Begin with the simplest models, which appear first. Have fun.

The Fundamentals

1. Follow the instructions step by step. Do not skip any steps.

2. Study the drawing and read the instructions. Remember that **the result of a given instruction is always shown in the next instructional step.** Compare an instruction with its result to understand what is required.

3. In origami, a section of paper is either folded in front **(valley fold)**, or it is folded behind **(mountain fold)**, and/or it is unfolded. These folds are the basis of all folds.

4. In origami, there are standard combinations of valley and mountain folds. In this book, they are referred to as *combination folds*. Each combination fold requires a folding procedure involving several steps. When a combination fold is specified in a step of a model's instructions, the required folding procedure is **not shown**. In this book, the step-by-step folding procedure is provided in the guide, *Combination Folds*.

5. The edges and folds of a model in the instructional drawings are not always perfectly aligned in order to show the folds or layers beneath. Always align the edges and folds according to the given instructions.

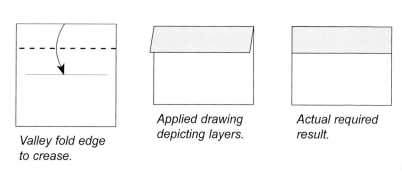

Valley fold edge
to crease.

Applied drawing
depicting layers.

Actual required
result.

6. Drawings of models with flaps often depict the distribution of the flaps and not the total number of flaps. For example, the popular model base shown on the right actually has eight flaps. The drawing depicts four layers of flaps on one side. Since there are eight flaps, you are to conclude that the flaps are evenly distributed with four on each side. Note: The example shown also defines a *section*, as well as a *flap*.

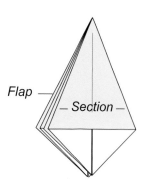

7. To Fold:

A. Most folds are made between two points of reference involving edges, creases and/or points. Bring these reference points together in the direction of the arrow. (*Example 1*) If only one reference point is given, fold it in the direction of the arrow to the point indicated by the arrow. (*Example 2*)

B. Align all pertaining edges and creases.

C. Fold firmly to produce a well-defined crease. When it pertains, fold precise points.

Example 1

Valley fold edges to center.* Align edges together on center line.* Fold a precise point. Set folds.

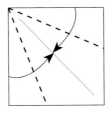

Example 2

Valley fold point down. Refer to the result to reproduce a proportionate fold. Align center lines.* Set fold.

* In this book, a crease that runs through the center of your paper, model, or a section thereof is referred to as the center line, or the center.

Steps and Drawings

- **The Instructional Step.** An intructional step features the instructions to one or more required folds. It also displays the result of the instructional step directly before it. All instuctional steps are numbered.

- **The Intermediate Step.** An intermediate step is used to clarify the process between a given instruction and its result. It is always preceded by a number and a lower case letter.

- **The Enlarged Drawing.** Drawings may be enlarged to clarify instructions. Significant enlargements are noted by the letter *E*. Slight enlargements are not noted.

- **The Magnified Drawing.** Outlined areas indicate that the area is magnified in the following step(s). The entire drawing of a magnified step is outlined.

LINES, ARROWS & SIMPLE FOLDS

Key to Lines

—————— **Edge**	———— **Existing Crease**
– – – – – – – **Valley Fold**	·················· **X-ray Outline** *Unseen edge.*
–·–·–·–·– **Mtn. Fold**	·················· **X-ray Guide** *Unseen fold.*

Valley fold *Fold in front.*

OR

Unfold or Pull Out

Unfold.

Pull Out.

Book fold *Fold flap(s) over.*

Mtn. fold *(Mountain fold) Fold behind.*

To mtn. fold either:

Turn over.   *Valley fold.*   *Turn over.*

OR

Valley fold   *Fold section*
required fold.   *behind.*

Learn Origami

  Fold; unfold *Establish crease.*

Fold; unfold.   *Valley fold.*   *Unfold.*

 Touch fold *Mark w/ a finger-width crease.*

Press here.

▶ **Open here** *Open layer or model.*

Open layer.

Open model.

▷ Push here, Push in, or Round

Push here.
Push in.

Round.

▷ Sink Fold *See Combination Fold.*

⟶ Indicates *Indicates important fold, point, crease, or edge.*

Lift *Lift flap or section perpendicular.*

Rotate paper/model

Rotate 45°.

Rotate 90°.

Turn paper/model over

Turn over
in direction
of arrow.

Turn over
in direction
of arrow.

Symbols

E   Enlarged Drawing *Drawing of model is larger than previous drawing.*

○   **Press, Hold, or Pinch Here**

COMBINATION FOLDS

These folds feature standard combinations of simple folds. Follow the procedure for each combination fold when it is specified in the model instructions.

The Preliminary Fold

Example:

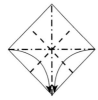

Preliminary Fold.

Procedure:

1.

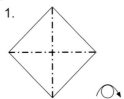

Start w/ mtn. folds.*
Turn paper over.

2.

3.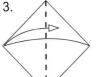

Steps 2 & 3: Valley fold corner to corner; unfold.

4.

**Turn paper
back over.**

5.

6.

Steps 5 & 6: Valley fold edge to edge; unfold.

7.

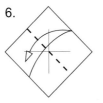

If center point is projected, press it inward. Fold sides in & down on creases.

a. *Drawings are enlarged*

Intermediate Step

Result

To check if your paper is a perfect square, always start by folding it in half, corner to corner. Edges should match exactly with precise folded points.

Squash Fold

Example:

Squash fold.

Procedure:

1.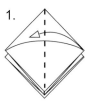

Establish crease
if needed.

2.

Lift flap & open.

Align flaps
& hold in
place. Align
center lines
& flatten.

3.

Result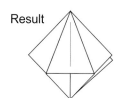

Note: When squash folding all flaps, keep center edges of all flaps aligned. Keep flaps as evenly distributed as possible.

Petal Fold

Example:

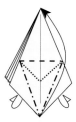

Petal fold.

Procedure:

1.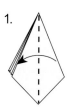

2.

Start w/ mtn. folds.
1. Book fold one flap over.
2. Valley fold edge to center.

3. 4. 5. Result

3. Unfold. Return flap. Repeat Steps 1-3 on the left.
4. Valley fold pt. to pt. between indicated pts.
5. Fold sides in. Stretch flap up to align sides on center.

Petal Fold II

Example: **Procedure:**

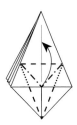   1. 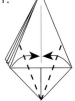   2.

Petal fold.   Valley fold edges   Unfold.
                          to center.

3. 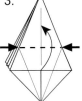   3a.    Result

Valley fold center pt. of edge up between indicated pts.
Valley fold sides in. Gently stretch flap up to align sides
on center line.

Rabbit Ear Fold

Example: **Procedure:**

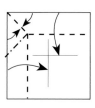

Rabbit ear fold.

1.

Valley fold; unfold.

2.

Valley fold; unfold.

3.

4.

Result

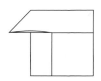

3. Fold section in half. Refold sides in.
4. Valley fold over. (Shown as mtn. fold in example.)

Pre-crease   *See also Pre-crease All Sections.*

Example: **Procedure:**

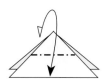

Pre-crease.
*Establish required crease
on both sides.*

1.

Valley fold.

2.

Mtn. fold behind.

3.

Unfold.

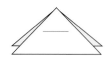

Result

Inside Reverse Fold / Outside Reverse Fold

Example: **Procedure:**

Inside reverse fold.

1.

Optional:
Pre-crease.

2.

Open layers.

3.

View of required creases,

Result

Push here to fold section between
layers. Refold model to complete fold.

Example: **Procedure:**

Outside reverse fold.

1.

Pre-crease.

2.

Open here.
Partially unfold.

3.

Result

Valley fold section back on creases.
Refold model to complete fold.

Pleat Fold

Example:

Pleat fold.

Arrow indicates required edge configuration.

Procedure:

Establish either fold first. Example shows:
1. Valley fold.
2. Valley fold. (Shown as mtn. fold in example.)

1.

2.

Result

Pre-crease <u>All</u> Sections

Example:

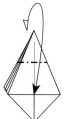

Pre-crease all sections.
Establish required crease on all sections.

Procedure:
On the common base shown, begin with flaps evenly distributed.

1. Pre-crease:
   a. Valley fold as shown.

b. Mtn. fold crease.
c. Unfold mtn. fold.

2.

3.

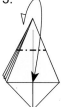

Result

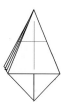

2. Book fold over two flaps from the right & two from behind on the left.
3. Repeat pre-crease.

Open Sink Fold / Closed Sink Fold

Example:

Open sink fold.

1.

2.

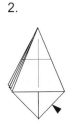

Procedure:
1. Pre-crease **all** sections.
2. Open model completely.
3. Flatten section within mtn. folds. Define mtn. folds.
4. Invert pt. as you refold model. Pinch & pleat flaps to refold. Note: valley folds are mtn. folds within new edges & vice versa.

3.

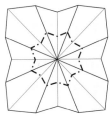

4.

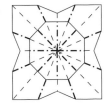

5. Result

Example:

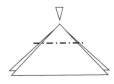

Closed sink fold.

Procedure:

1.

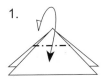

Pre-crease.

2.

Open top layer.

3.

Result

Invert section between top & next layer.

The Aloha Shirt

The Aloha Shirt

The Aloha Shirt displays one side of the paper. (Do <u>not</u> place paper with prints upside down; keep prints in proper position when paper is turned over.)

Scissors are required.

Model Description

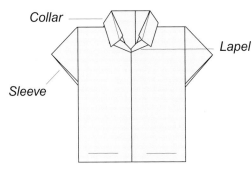

Collar

Lapel

Sleeve

1.

Begin with the desired side down. Valley fold corner to corner; unfold. Repeat.

Valley fold corners to center.

OPTIONAL: Unfold flaps & cut on creases to remove sections.

2.

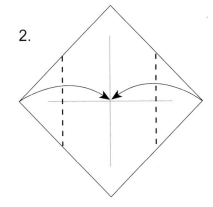

3.

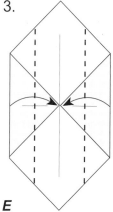

E

Valley fold edges
to center.

4.

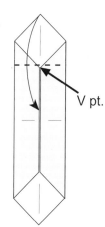

V pt.

Valley fold slightly
above V pt.

5.

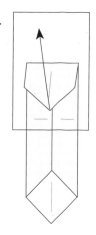

Lift flap
perpendicular.

6.

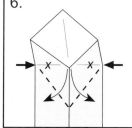

Valley fold center
corner pts. down.
Begin each valley fold
at indicated corner pt.
Align creases marked x
on edges.

7.

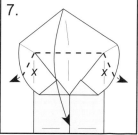

Valley fold pt. down.
Fold sides out to form
sleeves

Note: Creases marked x.

The Aloha Shirt

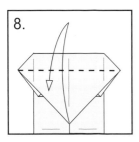

8.

Valley fold up between
pts. of sleeves; unfold.

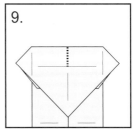

9.

Cut on center line
to crease of Step 8.

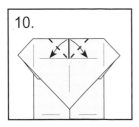

10.

Valley fold corners
to crease. **Unfold.**

11.
Valley fold pt. up.
Note: Fold determines
collar's width.

12.
Mtn. fold edge
behind. **Turn model
over.**

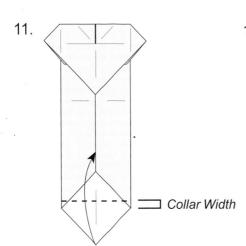

11.

Collar Width

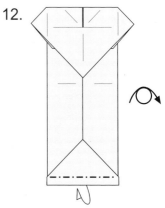

12.

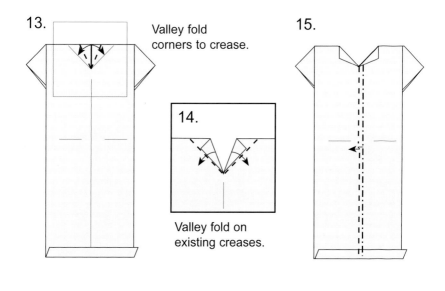

13. Valley fold corners to crease.

14. Valley fold on existing creases.

15.

15.
Pleat fold:

Valley fold edge to edge.

Valley fold side over. (15a)

16.
Valley fold edge to collar. Do not crease.

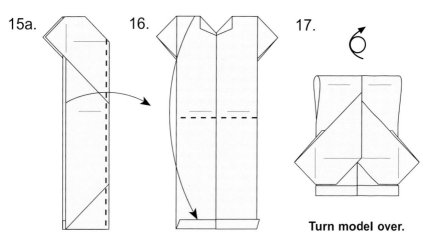

15a.

16.

17. Turn model over.

18.

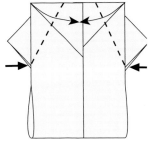

Valley fold corners to center.
Note position of center. Start
folds at indicated pts.

19.

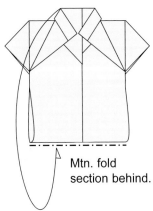

Mtn. fold
section behind.

20.

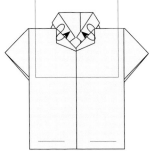

Tuck corners
under collar.

21.

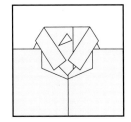

Push lightly on
each edge to splay
collar.

The Volcano *(Lua Pele)*

The Volcano (Lua Pele)

The Volcano is comprised of two models, *The Crater* and *The Eruption*. Each model requires one sheet of paper.

Use a 5:3 ratio (i.e., a 5-inch square for *The Crater* and a 3-inch square for *The Eruption*).

Model Description

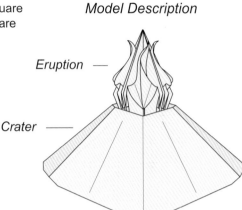

Eruption —

Crater —

The Crater

The Crater displays one side of the paper.
With the desired side down, begin with the Preliminary Fold.

1.

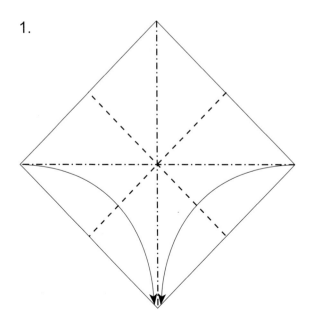

The Volcano

2.

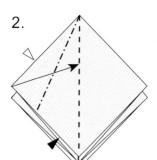

Squash fold each flap.

3.

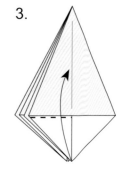

Valley fold flap up.

4.

Pre-crease **all** sections. Unfold completely with desired side down.

5.

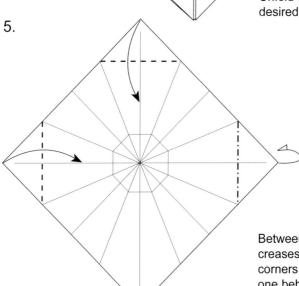

Between edge pts. of creases, valley fold two corners in & mtn. fold one behind.

6.

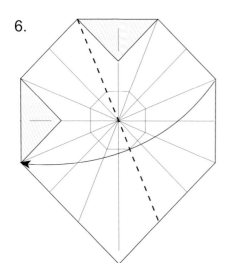

Valley fold corner to corner.

7.

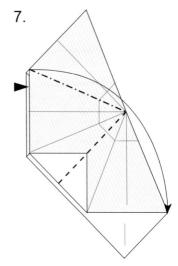

Fold corner to corner on existing creases.

8.

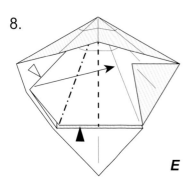

E

Squash fold flap.

9.

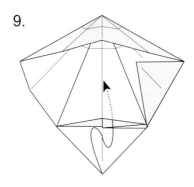

Valley fold section up between layers.

10.

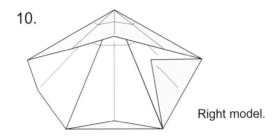

Right model.

11.

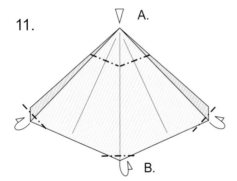

A. Close sink fold on existing creases of Step 4.
B. Mtn. fold all 5 corners under.

Result

The Eruption

The Eruption displays one side of the paper. Begin with the desired side down. **Proceed through Step 2 of *The Volcano*.**

3. Book fold a flap from the top & one from behind.

4. Petal fold all flaps.

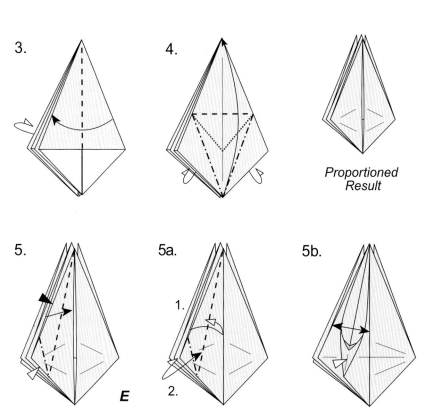

3.

4.

Proportioned Result

5.

E

5a.

1.

2.

5b.

Modified squash fold:
1. Valley fold edges of flap to center; unfold. (5a)
2. Pre-crease edge to now-existing crease. (5a)
3. Lift flap on valley fold & open.
4. Stretch layers apart at opening & flatten on pre-creases. (5b)

The Volcano

6.

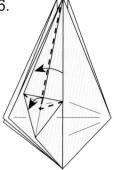

Valley fold flap over
to fold center pt. of
edge down.

7.

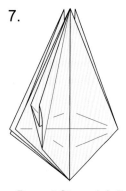

Repeat Steps 4 & 5
on all flaps.

8.

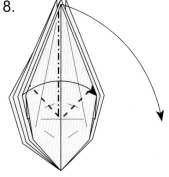

9.

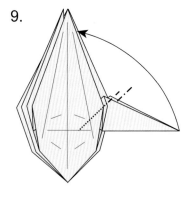

8.
Valley fold sides together
to reverse fold flap down.

9.
Inside reverse fold flap
up. Do not crease. Keep
fold rounded. Repeat
Steps 7 & 8 on
all flaps.

The Volcano

10.

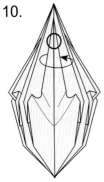

Note: Model is rotated.
Pinch & twist flaps to curl.

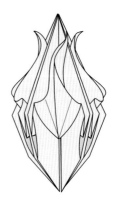

Place model in crater.

The Humuhumunukunukuāpuaʻa
(State Fish)

The Humuhumunukunukuāpuaʻa

The Humuhumu displays one side of the paper. With the desired side down, begin with the Preliminary Fold.

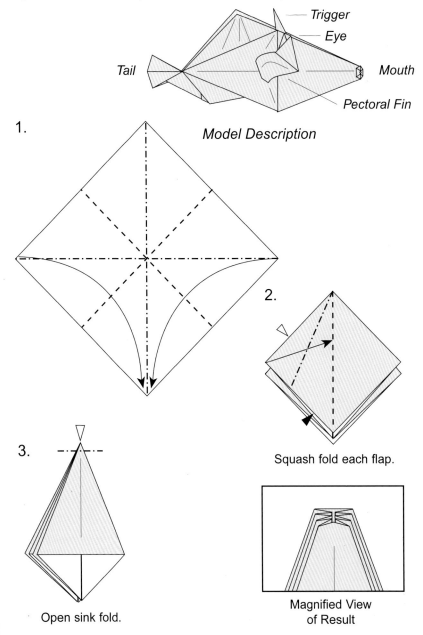

Trigger

Eye

Tail

Mouth

Pectoral Fin

Model Description

1.

2.

Squash fold each flap.

3.

Open sink fold.

Magnified View
of Result

The Humuhumunukunukuāpuaʻa

4.

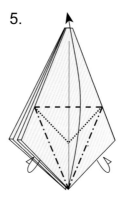

Evenly distribute flaps.
Book fold a flap from the
top & one from behind.

5.

Petal fold all
sections.

6.

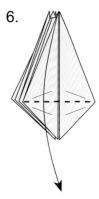

Valley fold a flap
down for the tail.

7. *E*

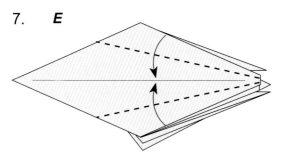

Model has been rotated.
Valley fold sides in.

8.

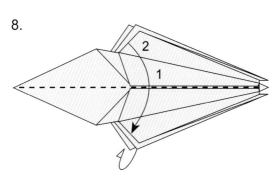

Evenly distribute flaps. Book fold two
flaps from the top & two from behind.

The Humuhumunukunukuāpuaʻa

9.

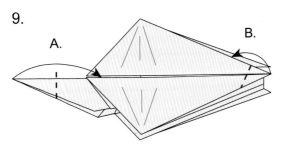

A. Valley fold pt. of tail beyond end pt. of body.
B. Valley fold pt. to edge.

10.

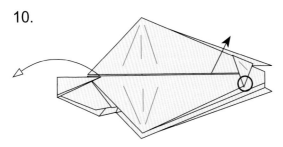

A. Unfold tail.
B. Pinch corner of flap. Lift layer.

11.

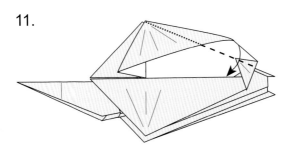

Refold side down. Repeat Steps 9B,
10B & 11 behind. Match sides.

The Humuhumunukunukuāpua'a

12.

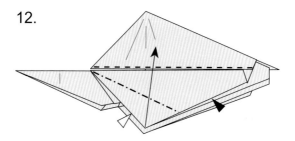

Modified squash fold. See 12a & 12b.
Repeat behind.

12a.

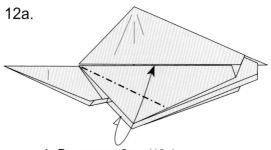

1. Pre-crease flap. (12a)
2. Lift & open flap.

12b.

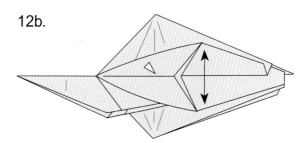

3. Stretch layers apart at the opening
   & flatten on pre-creases. (12b)

The Humuhumunukunukuāpua'a

13.

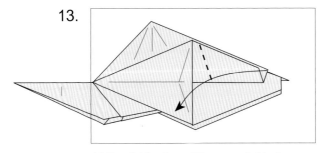

Valley fold edge of flap parallel to lower edge. Repeat behind. Match folds.

14.

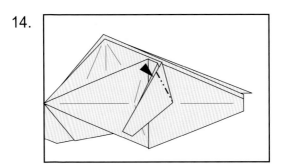

Stagger top layer to create an eye.

15.

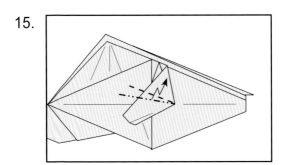

Pleat fold to form a fin. Repeat Steps 14 & 15 behind. Match sides.

The Humuhumunukunukuāpuaʻa

16.

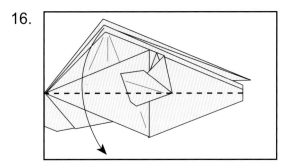

Book fold two flaps down. Do not set fold.

17.

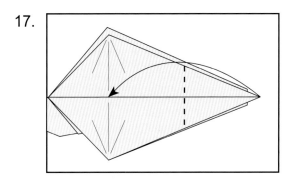

Valley fold pt. to crease.

18.

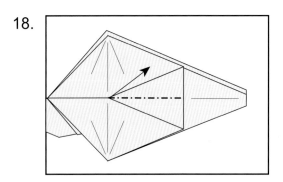

Lift flap. Pinch to mtn. fold in half.

The Humuhumunukunukuāpuaʻa

19.

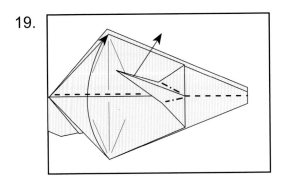

Continue to lift flap while refolding side up. Raise & align trigger as shown in next step. Compress layers to set folds.

20.

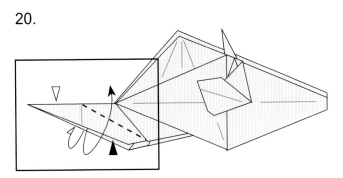

Outside reverse fold tail.

The Humuhumunukunukuāpuaʻa

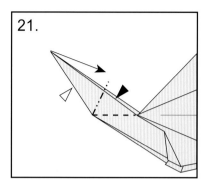

21.
Squash fold.

22.
OPTIONAL: Skip this step if only one side (side now showing) will be seen.

Valley fold tip behind to turn tail inside out.

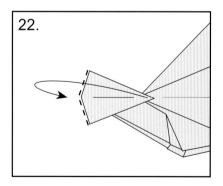

The Humuhumunukunukuāpuaʻa

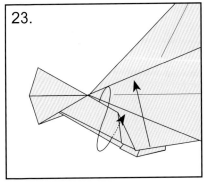

23.

Lift section to tuck edge under.
Repeat behind. Pt. of tail is also
tucked under.

24.

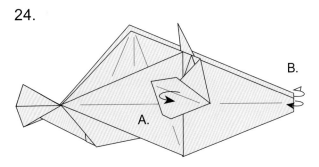

A. Curve fins outward.
B. Fold edges back to form the mouth.

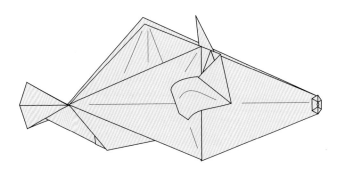

The Anthurium

The Anthurium

The Anthurium displays both sides of the paper. The heart-shaped spathe exhibits one side and the spadix exhibits the other. Select paper with contrasting sides.

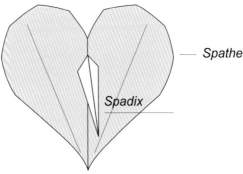

Spathe

Spadix

Model Description

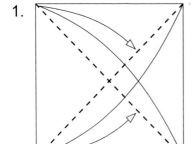

1.
Begin with the color of the spadix up. Valley fold corner to corner; unfold. Repeat.

2.
Mtn. fold edge behind to edge; unfold. Repeat.

3.
Collapse on creases into the Waterbomb Base.

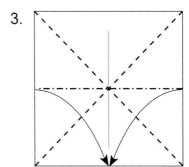

The Anthurium

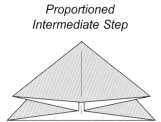

*Proportioned
Intermediate Step*

4.

E

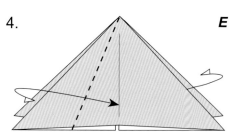

Pre-crease alternating flaps.

5.

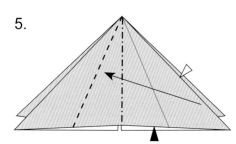

Squash fold.
Note: Open flap on
creases of Step 4.

Valley fold pt. to pt.
Repeat Steps 5 & 6
on flap behind.

6.

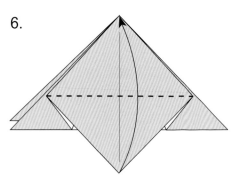

7.

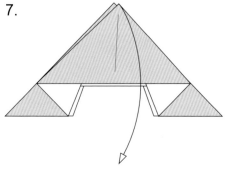

Unfold front flap only.

The Anthurium

8.

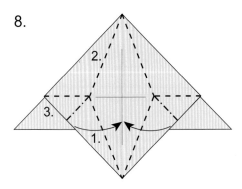

Fold in order shown:
1. Valley fold lower edges to center.
2. Valley fold sides to center. (8a)
3. Valley fold corner pts. down. (8a)

8a.

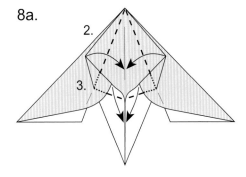

Open sides. Avoid creasing.
Fold flap up & back on
existing crease.

9.

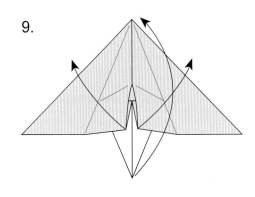

10.

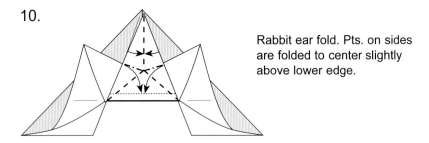

Rabbit ear fold. Pts. on sides are folded to center slightly above lower edge.

OPTIONAL: Higher spadix. Use for variation when folding several anthuriums.

Rabbit ear fold. Sections of sides are folded to lower edge.

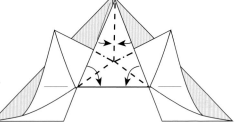

11.

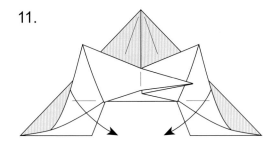

Close sides.
Rotate model.

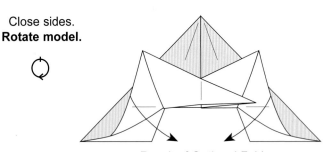

Result of Optional Fold

12.

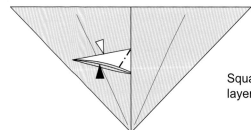

Squash fold. Note: Center layer is placed to one side.

13.

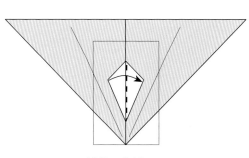

Valley fold over.

14.

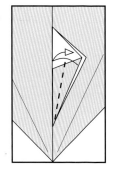

Valley fold edge to edge; unfold.

15.

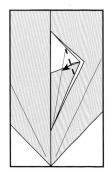

15.
Valley fold corner to crease.

16.
Valley fold edge to crease.

16.

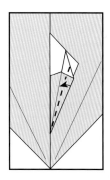

17.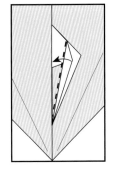

17.
Refold edge to center.

18.
Valley fold flap over.
Repeat Steps 13-18
on right side.

18.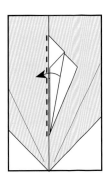

19. **Turn model over.**

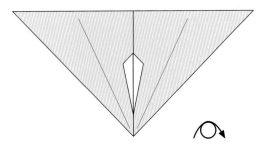

20.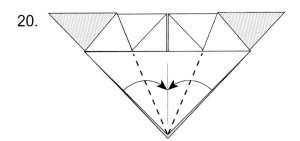

Valley fold edges in to center.

Steps 21-25 are optional. They form a
stem-like holder.

21.

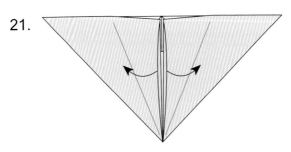

Open sides of top layer.

22.

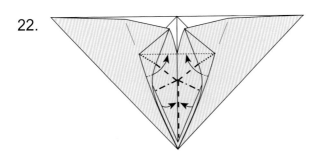

Rabbit ear fold inside flap.

23.

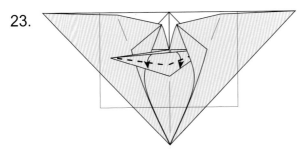

Valley fold edge to lower edge on
both sides of holder.

The Anthurium

24.

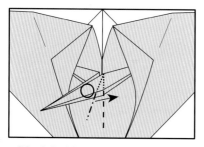

Pinch holder near base. Push straight down to pleat fold middle ridge.

25.

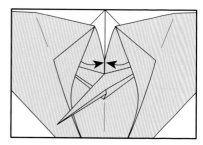

Refold sides to center.

26.

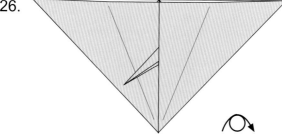

Turn model over.

27.

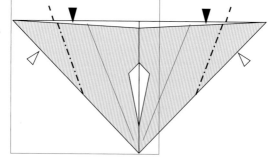

Inside reverse fold both sides.

28.

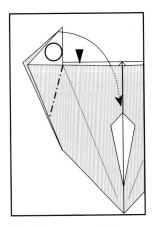

28a.

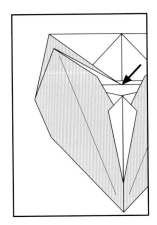

Inside reverse fold:
1. Pre-crease.
2. Open sides.
3. Pinch flap. Pull in & down until open edges of flap intersect the indicated inside edge at center line. (28a) Surpass pre-creases if necessary.
4. Close sides.

Repeat on the right side.

29.

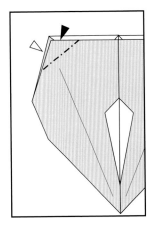

29a.

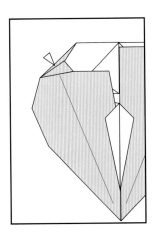

Inside reverse fold both edges as one:
1. Pre-crease.
2. Open corner pocket of **back** flap.
3. Push sections in on pre-creases. (29a)
4. Close sides.

Repeat on right side.

30.

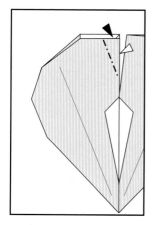

30a.

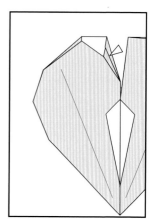

Inside reverse fold both edges as one:
1. Pre-crease.
2. Open corner pocket of **front** flap.
3. Push edges in on pre-creases. (30a)
4. Close sides.

Repeat on right side.

31.

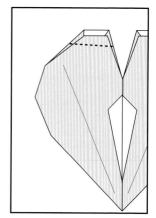

Inside reverse fold both edges of back flap creating a pocket.

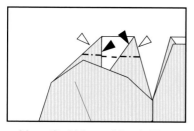

Magnified View of Back Flap

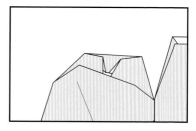

Result

32.

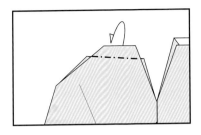

33.

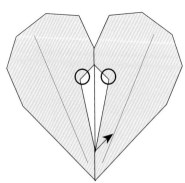

32.
Mtn. fold tab into pocket
behind. Repeat on right side.

33.
Slightly lift pt. of spadix.
Starting at the top, gently
pinch along edges to raise
center ridge. Unfold edges
within until they meet,
creating a five-sided cone.

Note: Use a toothpick to help
raise center ridge and to
unfold edges within.

34.

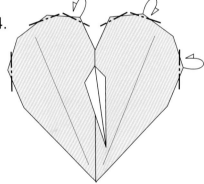

Curl edges behind to round
angles & create dimension.

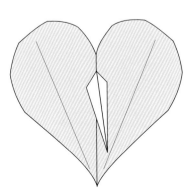

The Hibiscus *(Aloalo)*

The Hibiscus (Aloalo)

The Hibiscus displays both sides of the paper. The front of the model exhibits one side and the back exhibits both sides. Select either paper with similar sides OR paper with contrasting sides. Paper with contrasting sides provides an interesting and realistic effect.

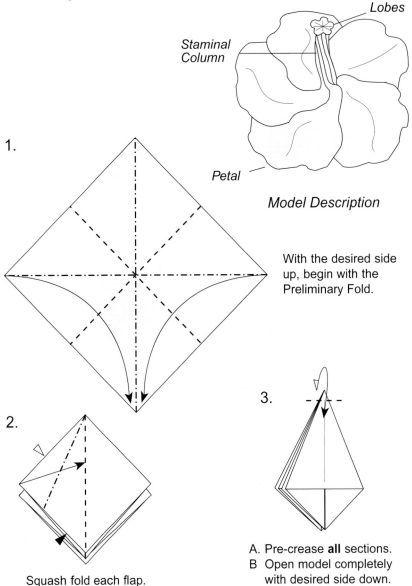

Lobes

Staminal Column

Petal

Model Description

With the desired side up, begin with the Preliminary Fold.

1.

2.

Squash fold each flap.

3.

A. Pre-crease **all** sections.
B Open model completely with desired side down.

The Hibiscus

4.

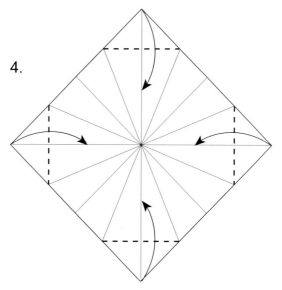

Valley fold corners in between
edge pts. of creases.

OPTIONAL: Unfold flaps & cut
on creases to remove sections.

5.

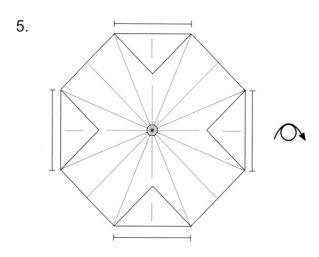

Turn model over.

The Hibiscus

Note the following:
1. Placement of flaps beneath.
2. Mtn. fold on existing creases.
3. Resulting petals are numbered.

6.

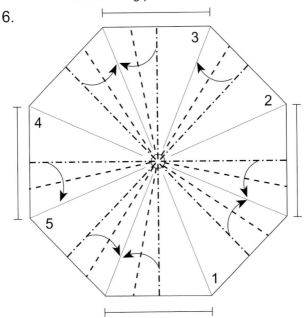

To begin, mtn. fold an edge. Valley fold edge to existing crease.
Release fold. Repeat 7 more times. **Raise center pt.** Reset all folds.
Use paper clips to hold folds.

7.

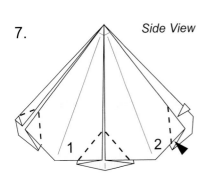

Side View

Inside reverse fold all corners
of petals.

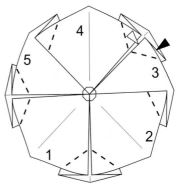

Top View
Note: Arrangement of full petals
(1,2 & 4) & half petals (3 & 5).

The Hibiscus

8.

Result

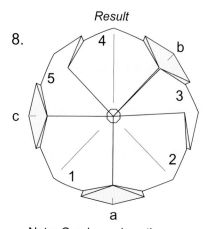

Note: Overlapped sections are labeled a, b & c.

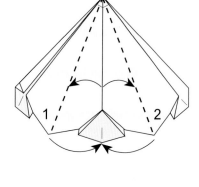

Valley fold flaps open. Pts. are folded under.

9.

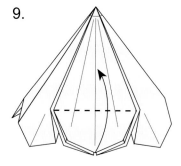

Valley fold up at widest pt.
1. Lift flap.
2. Press to secure lower edges in place. (9a)
3. Stretch flap up. Align indicated edges with creases behind. (9a)

9a.

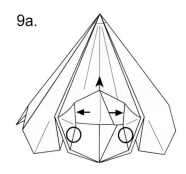

The Hibiscus

10.

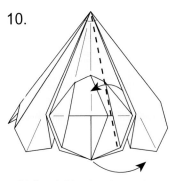

Valley fold edge to center.
Pt. is folded back out.

11.

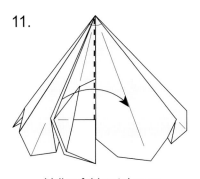

Valley fold petal open

12.

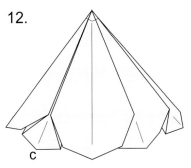

c

Repeat Steps 8-11 on sections
b & c. See Step 8 *Top View*.

13.

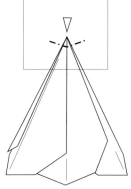

Flatten tip out on creases of Step 3. Insert the flat end of a pencil in model to help accomplish this fold.

Magnified Result

14.

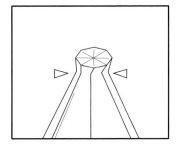

14.
Unfold overlapping layers within edges of current fold.

OPTIONAL: To create the rounded lobes seen in the presentation models, turn model upside down & place 5 small, slightly flattened foil or paper balls in the tip. Press sides in to lock in place.

15.

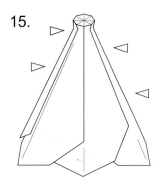

Start at the top. Neatly & tightly compress sides in to at least half the length of model. Arrange overlaps & smooth petals.

16.

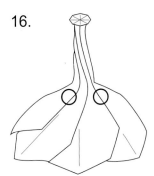

Pinch model below base of
staminal column. Push
down to splay petals.

17.

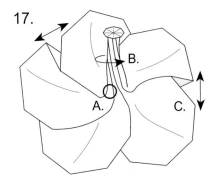

A. Hold base of column. Cup
   petals up.
B. Gently twist to tighten column.
C. Stretch to extend petal edge.

18.

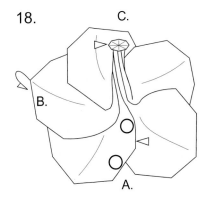

A. Press each petal at base of
   column. Pinch edge & twist
   up.
B. Curl points under.
C. Indent stamen to form lobes.

Shape petals as desired.

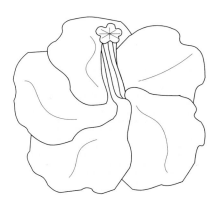

The Plumeria (Melia)

The Plumeria *(Melia)*

The Plumeria and *The Hibiscus* are similar in concept and procedure. Initial steps are shared. Refer to *The Hibiscus* to better understand *The Plumeria* if needed.

The Plumeria displays both sides of the paper. The front of the model exhibits one side and the back exhibits both sides. Select either paper with similar sides OR paper with contrasting sides. Paper with contrasting sides provides an interesting and realistic effect.

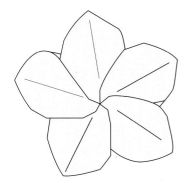

Proceed through Step 5 of the Hibiscus.

Note the following:
1. Placement of flaps beneath.
2. Mtn. fold on existing creases.
3. Resulting petals are numbered.

To begin, mtn. fold an edge. Valley fold edge to existing crease. Release fold. Repeat 7 more times. **Depress center pt.** Reset all folds. Use paper clips to hold folds.

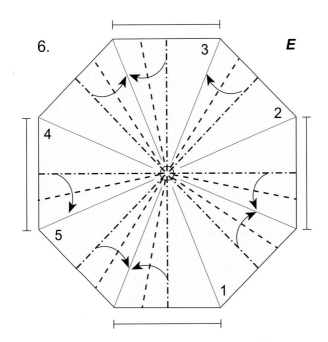

6.   E

7.

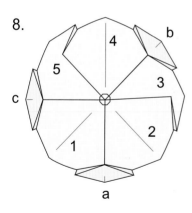

Inside reverse fold all corners of petals.

Note: Arrangement of full petals (1,2 & 4) & half petals (3 & 5).

Inside View

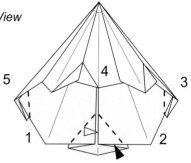

8.

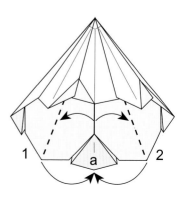

Note: Overlapped sections are labeled a, b & c.

Valley fold flaps open. Pts. are folded under.

The Plumeria

9.

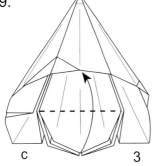

c   3

9a.

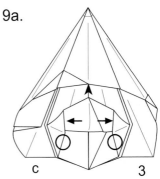

c   3

Valley fold up at widest pt:
1. Lift flap.
2. Press to secure lower edges in place. (9a)
3. Stretch flap up. Align indicated edges with creases behind. (9a)

10.

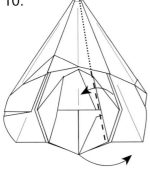

Valley fold edge to center.
Pt. is folded out.

11.

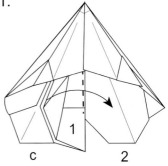

c   2

Valley fold petal open.

12.

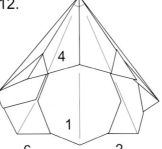

c   2

Repeat Steps 8-11 on sections
b & c. See Step 8 *Top View*.

The Plumeria

13.

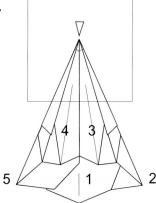

Magnified Result

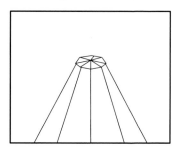

Flatten tip out on creases of Step 3. Insert the flat end of a pencil in model to help accomplish this fold.

OPTIONAL: To create the rounded end of the stem, turn model upside down & place a little cotton in the tip.

14.

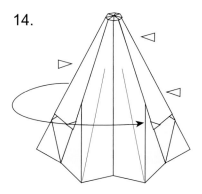

Neatly compress sides as you twist model in the direction of the overlaps. Compress & twist a stem to approx. half the length of the model.

The Plumeria

15.

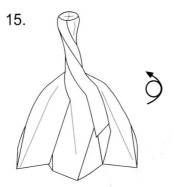

Turn model over.

16.

A.   B.

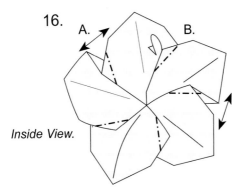

Inside View.

A. Stretch to extend petal edges.
Arrange overlaps.
B. Mtn. fold corners under to thin petals.

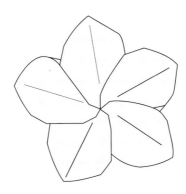

The Marlin (A'u)

The Marlin (A'u)

The Marlin displays both sides of the paper. The marlin's belly exhibits one side and the rest of the marlin exhibits the other. Select paper with contrasting sides.

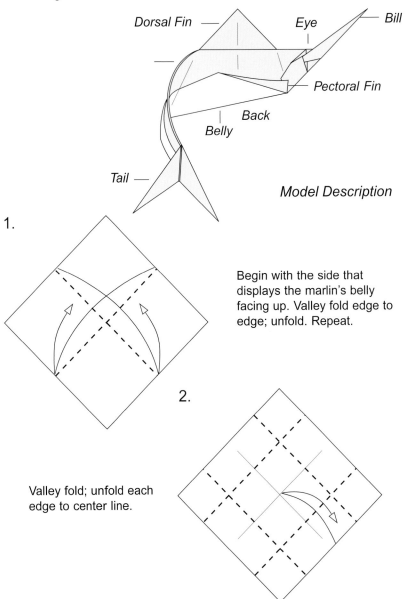

Dorsal Fin — Eye — Bill

Pectoral Fin

Back

Belly

Tail —

Model Description

1.

Begin with the side that displays the marlin's belly facing up. Valley fold edge to edge; unfold. Repeat.

2.

Valley fold; unfold each edge to center line.

The Marlin

3.

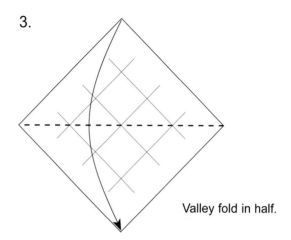

Valley fold in half.

4. *E*

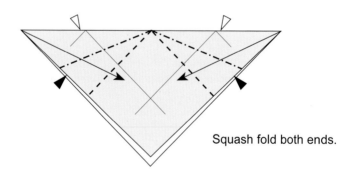

Squash fold both ends.

5.

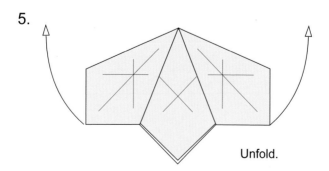

Unfold.

6.

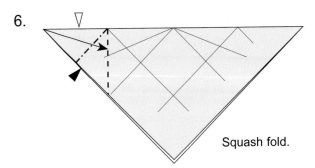

Squash fold.

7.

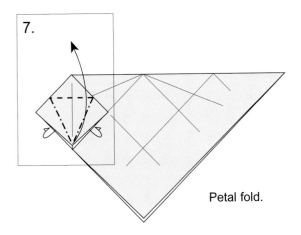

Petal fold.

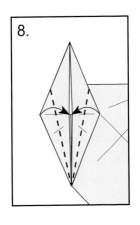

8.

8.
Valley fold edges to center.

9.
Valley fold edges to center. (Fold lies partially between layers.)

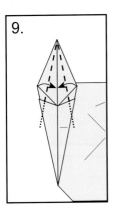

9.

The Marlin

10.

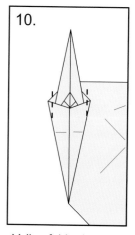

Valley fold edges in.

11.

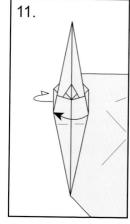

Flip head over.

12.

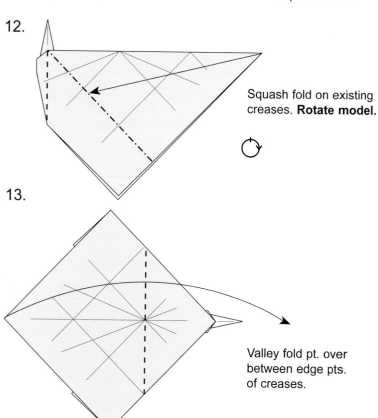

Squash fold on existing creases. **Rotate model.**

13.

Valley fold pt. over between edge pts. of creases.

14.

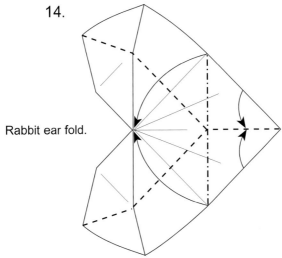

Rabbit ear fold.

15.

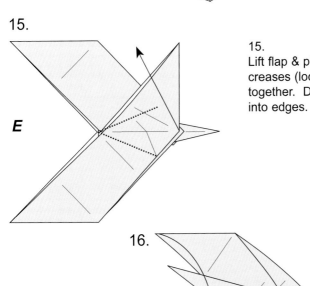

E

15.
Lift flap & pinch to bring
creases (located beneath)
together. Define creases
into edges.

16.

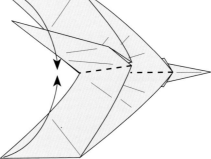

16.
Valley fold sides together.

17.

E

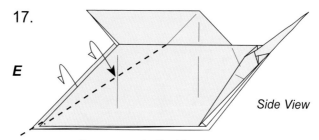

Side View

Pre-crease both sides between
end pt. & crease on dorsal fin.

18.

A.

B.

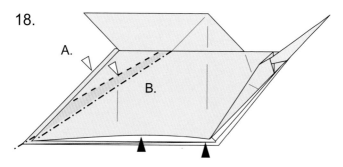

A. Close sink fold section behind on
   creases established in previous step.
B. Close sink fold (shaded section).
   See 18a.

18a.

B.

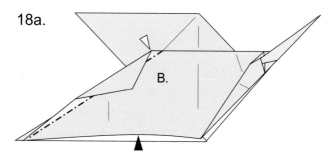

1. Valley fold over on top crease.
2. Open layers. (18a)
3. Close sink fold. Start at top pt.

The Marlin

19.

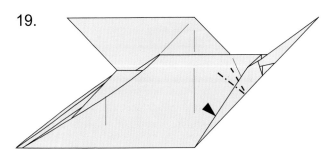

Pleat fin. Begin by mtn. folding
existing crease.

20.

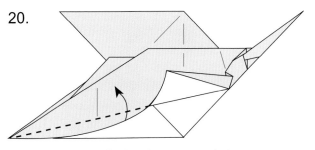

Valley fold up between end pts.
Repeat Steps 19 & 20 behind.

21.

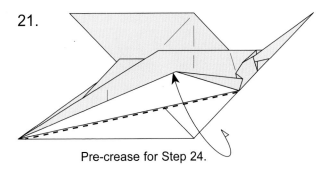

Pre-crease for Step 24.

The Marlin

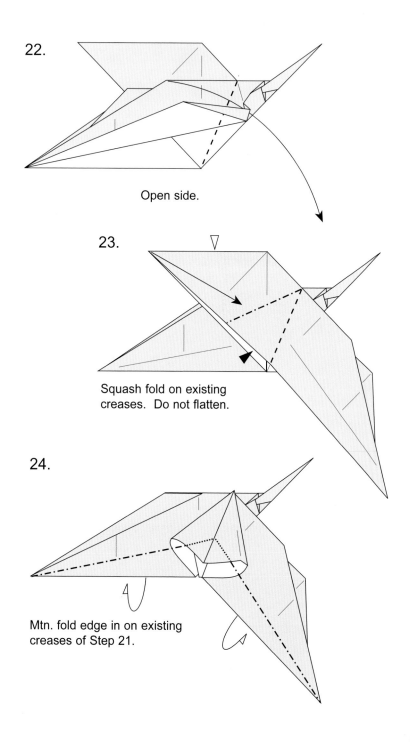

22.

Open side.

23.

Squash fold on existing
creases. Do not flatten.

24.

Mtn. fold edge in on existing
creases of Step 21.

25. Fold sides back together.

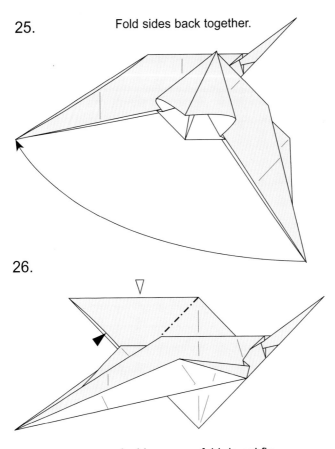

26.

Inside reverse fold dorsal fin.

27.

B.

A.

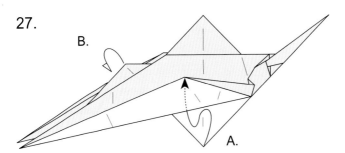

A. Valley fold up under top layer.
B. Mtn. fold tab into pocket
behind to lock sides together.

The Marlin

28.

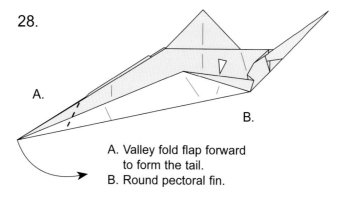

A.

B.

A. Valley fold flap forward
   to form the tail.
B. Round pectoral fin.

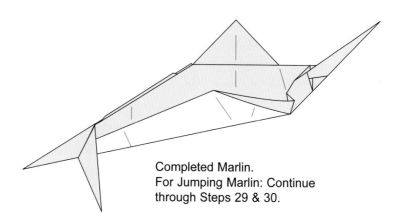

Completed Marlin.
For Jumping Marlin: Continue
through Steps 29 & 30.

29.

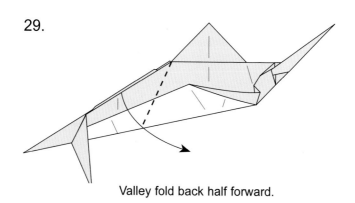

Valley fold back half forward.

30.

A.

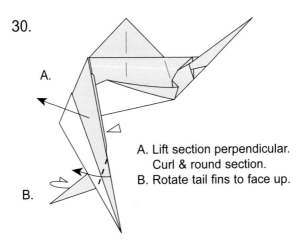

A. Lift section perpendicular.
   Curl & round section.
B. Rotate tail fins to face up.

B.

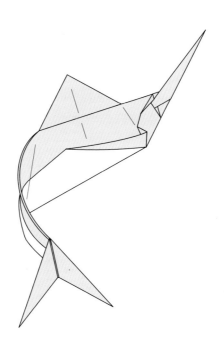

The Gecko (Mo'o 'alā)

The Gecko *(Mo'o 'alā)*

The Gecko displays one side of the paper. With the desired side down, begin with the Preliminary Fold.

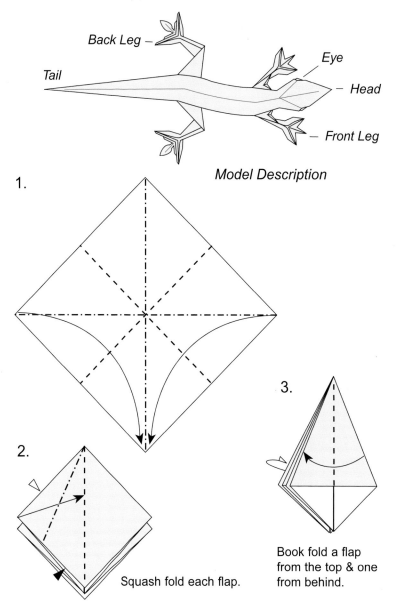

Model Description

2. Squash fold each flap.

3. Book fold a flap from the top & one from behind.

4.

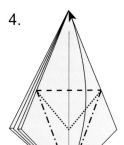

Petal fold three flaps.

5.

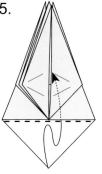

Valley fold section up between layers.

6.

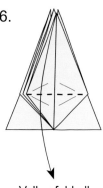

Valley fold all flaps down.

7.

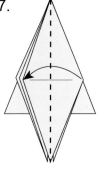

Book fold flap.

8.

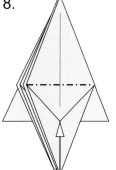

8a.

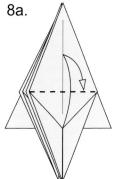

8.
Invert section:
1. Valley fold; unfold. (8a)
2. Pull open lower flaps.
3. Invert section while refolding model. (8b)

8b.

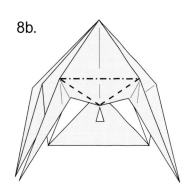

9.

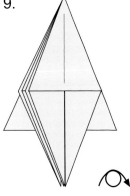

Invert remaining point.
Evenly distribute flaps.
Turn model over.

10.

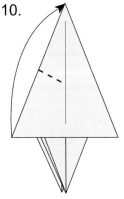

Valley fold
corner to pt.

11.

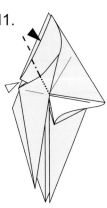

Inside reverse
fold.

12.

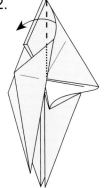

Valley fold edge out
from center line.

13.

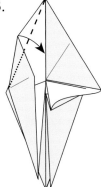

Valley fold
edge to center.

14.

Fold pt. to pt.
Mtn. fold center
section in half.

The Gecko

15.

16.

17.

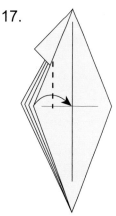

Repeat Steps 11-13 on right side. Note: Step 11 is shown.

Book fold flap.

Valley fold pt. to center. Crease only above existing crease.

18.

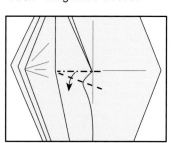

18.
Valley fold lower edge to center. Smooth excess paper to mid-pt. of flap. Pleat fold. (18a)

19.
Repeat Steps 17 & 18 on the right.

18a. *Magnified Section*

19.

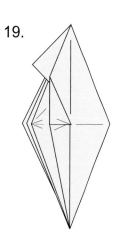

The Gecko

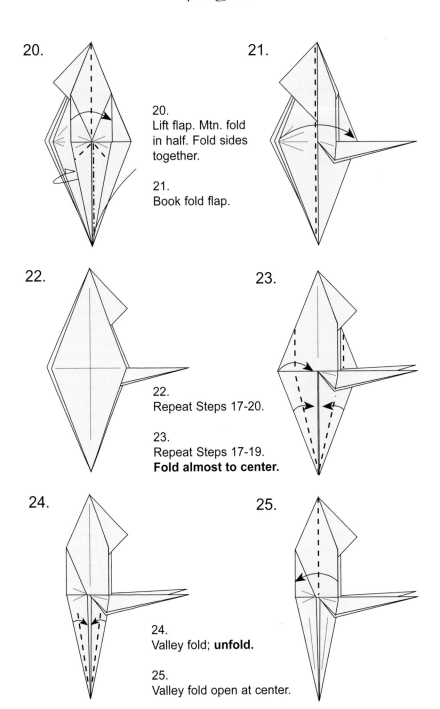

20.

20.
Lift flap. Mtn. fold in half. Fold sides together.

21.
Book fold flap.

21.

22.

22.
Repeat Steps 17-20.

23.
Repeat Steps 17-19.
Fold almost to center.

23.

24.

24.
Valley fold; **unfold.**

25.
Valley fold open at center.

25.

The Gecko

26.

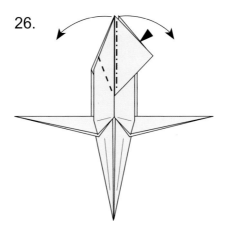

Mtn. fold along edges of
center flap. Valley fold
front legs out to open flap.

27.

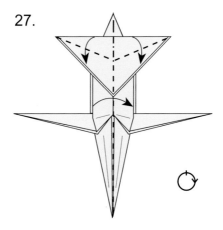

Valley fold top edge to
lower edges. Fold model
in half to complete fold.
Rotate model.

The Gecko

28.

Valley fold all legs in half; unfold.

29.

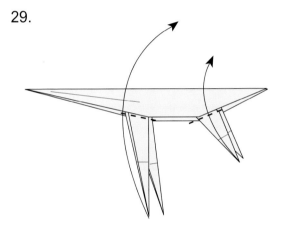

Valley fold legs up. Repeat behind.

30.

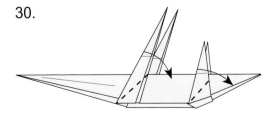

Valley fold legs forward. Repeat behind.

31.

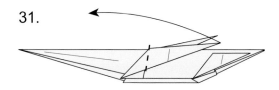

Valley fold rear leg back. Repeat behind.

32.

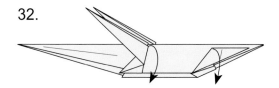

Right model. Let legs fall.

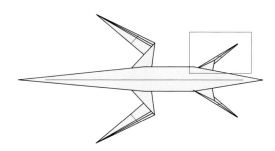

Front Legs Only

33.

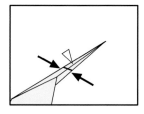

Open layers. Pinch
directly behind crease
(28) & hold thru Step 36.
Flatten middle fold.

34.

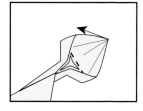

Compress section up to
valley fold at base of foot.

35.

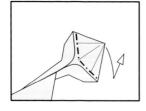

Mtn. fold section down;
unfold at right angle.

36.

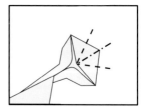

Mtn. fold section in half.
Fold sides of foot together
to complete fold.

37.

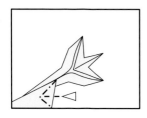

Push mid-pt. of edge in
to indent.

38.

Repeat Steps 33-37
on other front leg.

Back Legs

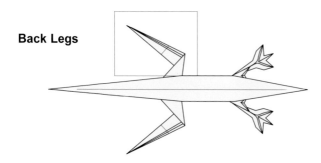

39.

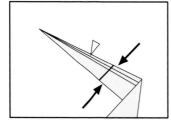

Open layers. Pinch directly
behind crease (28) & hold
thru Step 43. Flatten middle
fold.

40.

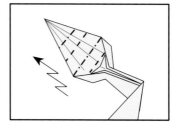

Compress section up to
valley fold at base of foot
then pleat fold.

The Gecko

41.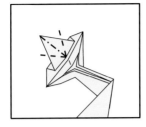

42.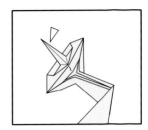

41.
Pinch in half to rabbit ear fold section.

43.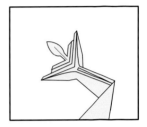

42.
Flatten end of center toe. Fold sides of foot together.

43.
Repeat Steps 39-42 on other back leg.

44.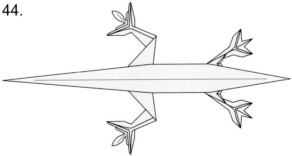

Side View

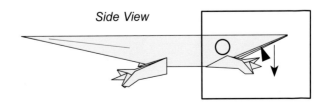

Pinch sides of model together. Separate four middle flaps. Pinch & pull downward.

45.

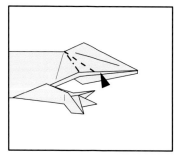 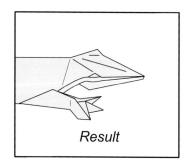

Result

Separate top layers. Pleat fold top layer
only to form eye. Repeat on other side.

46.

Curve model to hold sides together. Round tail by curving
lower edges under on existing creases of Step 24.

Top View

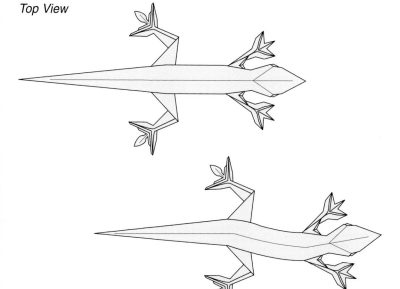

The Snow King Protea

The Snow King Protea

The Snow King Protea displays both sides of the paper. Select paper with contrasting sides OR paper with similiar sides that has been *spot layered*. Spot layering instructions follow.

Select paper at least 10 inches square.

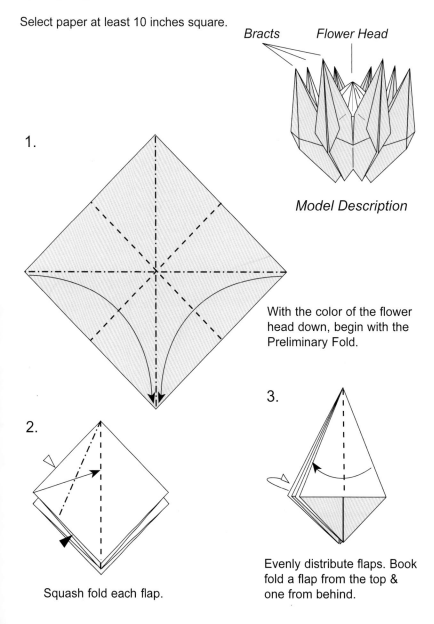

Bracts   Flower Head

Model Description

1.

With the color of the flower head down, begin with the Preliminary Fold.

2.

Squash fold each flap.

3.

Evenly distribute flaps. Book fold a flap from the top & one from behind.

The Snow King Protea

4.

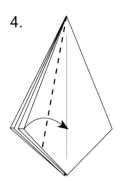

4.
Valley fold edge to center.

5.
A. Valley fold pt. to pt.; unfold.
B. Unfold flap.

5.

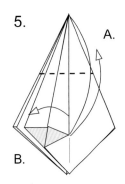

A.

B.

6.

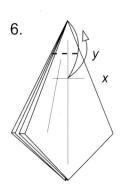

y

x

6.
Fold pt. to crease *x*; unfold.

7.
Pre-crease both *x* & *y* on **all** sections.

7.

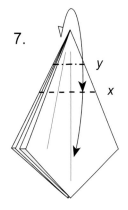

y

x

8.

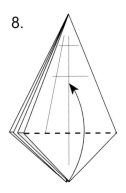

8.
Valley fold up. Repeat on all section

9.
Valley fold edges to center. Crease only below crease *x*; unfold. Repeat on all sections.

9.

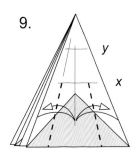

y

x

10.

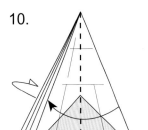

Book fold a flap from the
top & one from behind.

11.

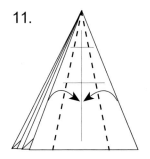

Valley fold edges to
center on all sections.

12.

Open model.

13.

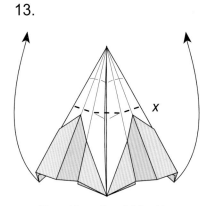

Roughly valley fold edges
up on crease x. Maintain
folds of Step 12.

14.

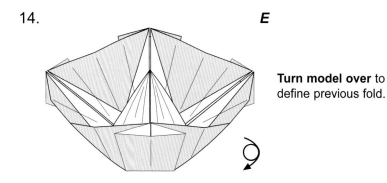

E

Turn model over to
define previous fold.

The Snow King Protea

15.

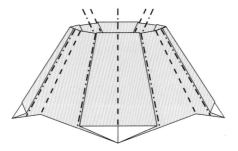

Pleat model on existing creases.

16.

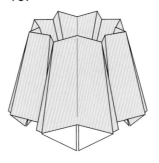

Turn model over.

17.

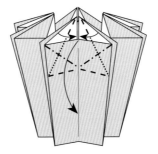

Petal fold all 8 sections.

The Snow King Protea

18.

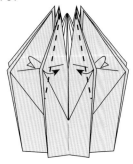

19.

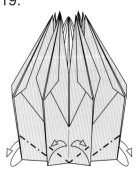

18.
On both sides of all pleats, fold edge in 1/3 of the
distance to center. **Unfold at a right angle.**

19.
See model results before proceeding.
OPTION 1: Fold corners to center on alternating
sections; unfold.
OPTION 2: Skip this step.

20.

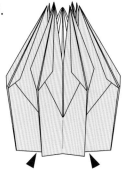

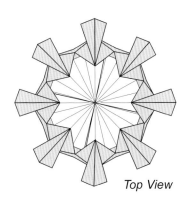

Top View

Place fingers within model to form central dome.
Gently stretch open center. Define crease *y* (Step 7)
to determine outer edges & diameter of dome.
Stretch apart <u>every other overlapping fold within
dome diameter only</u>. Retain a peak.

The Snow King Protea

21.

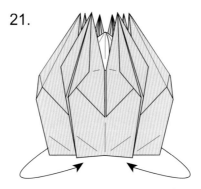

Grasp opposing lower pleats. Gently pull out and down to further stretch, shape & define center dome.

21.

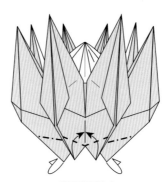

OPTION 1:
Refold corners on existing creases (Step 20). Paper clip corners to set folds if necessary. Reset pts. & bract creases.

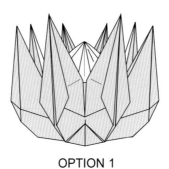

OPTION 1

22.

OPTION 2:
Glue sides of each pleat together
to close bottom. (If you plan to add
a stem, do not close bottom hole
completely.)

OPTIONAL STEM: Insert a paper-covered or painted dowel of the
appropriate size through the bottom hole of the model.

The Snow King Protea

Spot Layering Instructions

The insides of the bracts of *The Snow King Protea* exhibit both sides of the
paper. Compare the results of paper with contrasting sides to paper with
similar sides that has been spot layered.

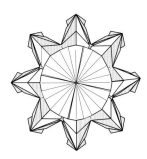

Contrasting Sides   *Spot Layered Paper*

The Snow King Protea

Read the section on *Layering*.

To spot layer paper for *The Snow King Protea*: Select paper with similar sides. Begin with the desired side up. Complete Steps 1-7 to determine crease *x* and crease *y*. Measure the approximate distance from the tip to the mid-pt. between crease *x* and *y*. Multiply the distance by two to arrive at the number of square inches of your spot layer. For example: the distance would measure 2 inches on a model folded from a 10-inch square sheet of paper. Therefore, the spot layer would be a 4-inch square.

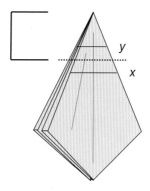

To fold your spot layer, begin with the desired side down. Complete Steps 1 & 2 of the general instructions for *The Snow King Protea*.

1.   2.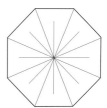

The Snow King Protea

1. Cut off lower sections to create an octagon.
2. Unfold spot layer.
3. Unfold model completely with desired side up.
4. Spray back of spot layer with adhesive.
5. Align center pt.,valley & mtn. folds. Adhere spot layer to base layer.
6. Refold. Reestablish crease *y* on all sections of spot layer. Continue with general instructions.

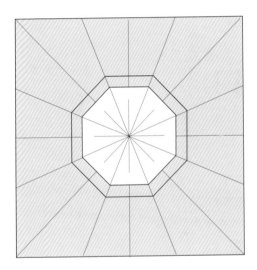

The Orchid ('Okika)

The Orchid ('Okika)

The Orchid offers two flower styles and two petal variations.

The Orchid displays both sides of the paper. The front of the orchid exhibits one side; the back of the orchid exhibits both sides. See Step 31 for an example of the back of *The Orchid*. Select paper with similar sides OR paper with contrasting sides. Paper with contrasting sides provides an interesting and realistic effect.

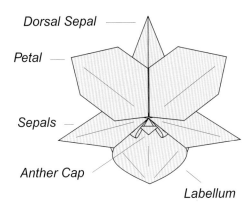

Dorsal Sepal

Petal

Sepals

Anther Cap

Labellum

Model Description

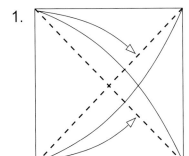

1. Begin with the desired side down. Valley fold corner to corner; unfold. Repeat.

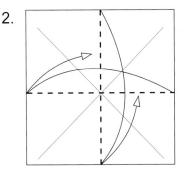

2. Valley fold edge to edge; unfold. Repeat.

The Orchid

3.

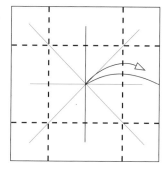

Valley fold; unfold each edge to center.

4.

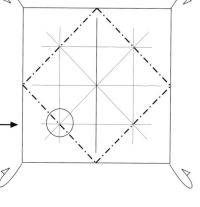

Mtn. fold each corner behind to center pt. **Unfold.** Note: Mtn. fold intersects existing creases.

5.

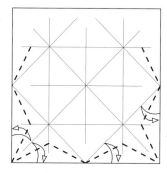

OPTIONAL: Pre-crease for *inside reverse folds.* See Step 7. Valley fold; unfold each section of edge to existing crease.

6.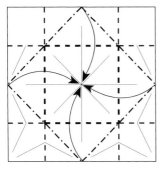

6a. *Intermediate Step*

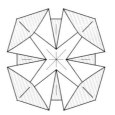

Fold midpoint of each edge to center. Collapse each corner in on existing creases.

7.

Proportioned Result

E

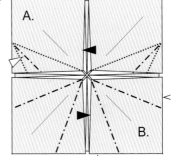

A. Petal Variation 1: Inside reverse fold at an offset:
  1. Open layers. Note: Lift top layer without creasing.
  2. Valley fold edge to center. (7a)
  3. Lower top layer. Bring section of edge outward. (7b)
  4. Determine desired angle of edge. (7c) Note: Several options are shown.
  5. Set folds.

B. Sepals: Inside reverse fold all edges.

The Orchid

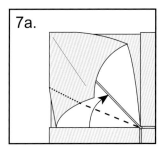

7a.

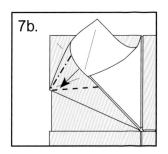

7b.

Left Petal Only

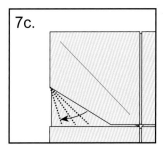

7c.

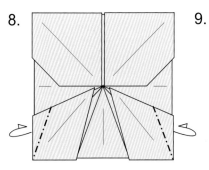

8.

Mtn. fold edge behind to center of sepal.

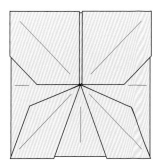

9.

Turn model over.

10.

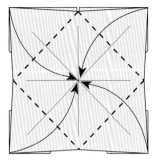

Valley fold corners to center.
Do not crease petals or sepals.

11.

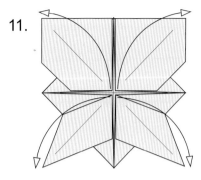

11.
Unfold.

12.
Note: Do not crease petals or sepals.
Fold *a* to *d*. Touch fold *b*.
Fold *f* to *d*. Touch fold *e*.
Fold *f* to *b*. Valley fold *c*
between creases.

12.

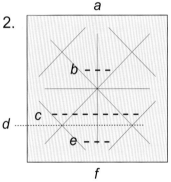

13.
Open petal flaps behind.
Lift section.

14.
Valley fold edge as shown
to imaginary line.

13.

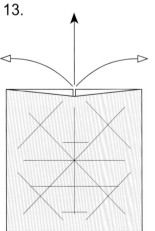

14.

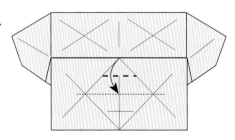

The Orchid

15.

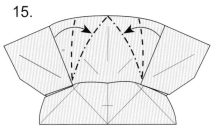

Temporarily release previous fold. Mtn.
fold existing creases. Valley fold petal
edges to new edges (mtn. folds).

16.

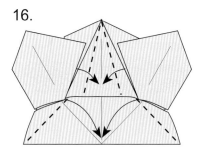

Valley fold all edges to center.
Note: Lower valley folds are existing.

17.

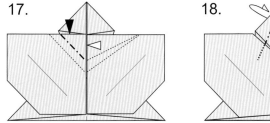

18.

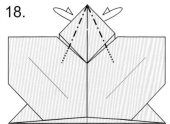

17.
Inside reverse fold. Repeat & match fold on right side. Note:
Several optional folds are shown.

18.
Mtn. fold behind. Fold will vary according to length & angle of folds
of Step 17. Flatten overlapping sections, if any. See Step 20 for
possible results.

The Orchid

19.

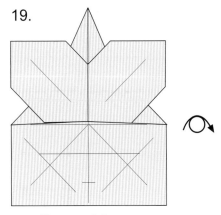

Turn model over.

20.

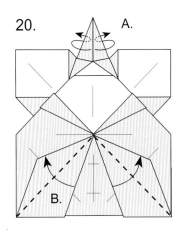

A.

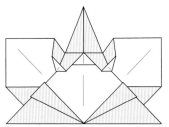

*Result with
Overlapping Sections*

A. OPTIONAL: Tuck in
   between layers.
B. Valley fold edges up.

21.

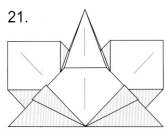

*Model is depicted
in sections.*

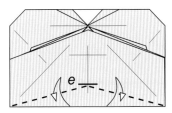

Valley fold; unfold between
mid-pt. of crease *e* of Step
12 & each corner pt.

22.

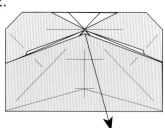

Lift section perpendicular.

23.

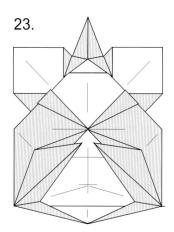

Turn model over.

24.

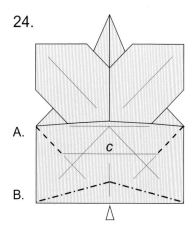

A.
Valley fold; unfold existing
creases as shown to help
determine the exact length
of crease c (Step 12).

B.
Push edge to mtn. fold
existing creases. Define
into an edge.

25.

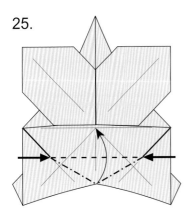

Note: Position of mtn. folds.

Valley fold edge up on crease *c*.
Align center lines. See Step 27
for front view of result.
Turn model over.

Pinch along edge between
indicated pts. to set fold.
Turn model over.

26.

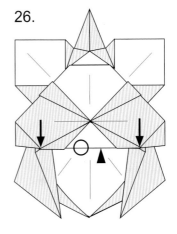

27.

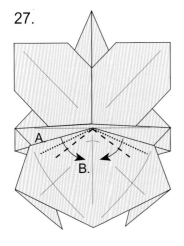

A. Roughly establish mtn. folds
   on layer behind top layer &
   between each indicated pt. in
   Step 25 & pt. of peak.
B. Valley fold edges down
   towards but <u>not</u> to center line.
   Set mtn. folds of Step A.

The Orchid

28.

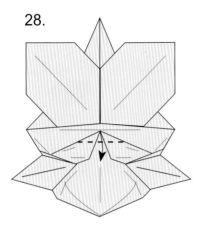

Valley fold tip down to create anther cap.

Push & hold each edge down to round while valley folding each corner to center on existing creases.

29.

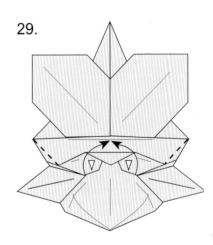

30.

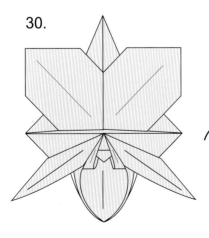

ORCHID STYLE 1

Turn model over.

The Orchid

31.

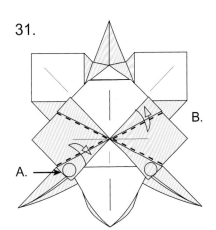

A. Pinch tabs to set folds of Step 29.
B. Valley fold; unfold along each folded edge. Do not crease petals.

Fold midsections in half. Center pt. is folded inward.

32.

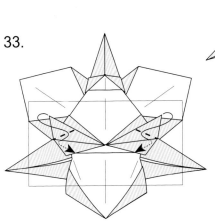

33.

Valley fold tabs into pockets to lock model.
OPTIONAL: Fold sections into pockets above. (33a)
Turn model over.

Magnified Section

Magnified Result

33a.

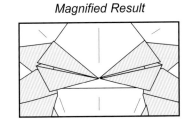

34.

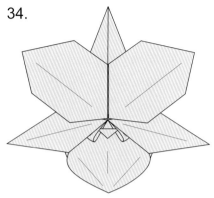

Shape model. Curl sepals, round labellum, etc. See presentation models.

ORCHID STYLE 2

Follow the general instructions through Step 31A; then:

Valley fold midsections in half. Center pt. is folded inward. Overlap petals onto sepals.

32.

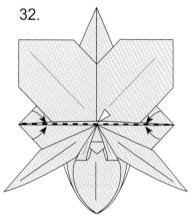

33.

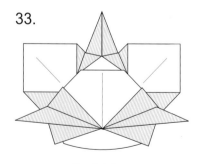

Back View

Lock model. See Orchid Style 1, Step 33.

34.

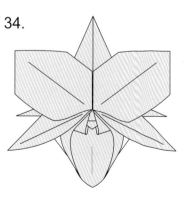

Shape model. See presentation models.

PETAL VARIATION 2

Follow the general instructions to Step 4.

OPTIONAL:
Pre-crease for inside reverse folds. See Step 7. Valley fold; unfold each section of edge to existing crease.

Proceed through Step 6.

5.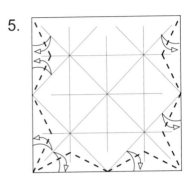

7.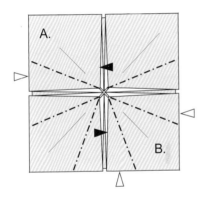

8.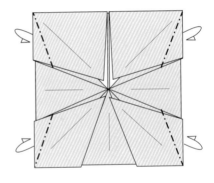

7.
A. Petals: Inside reverse fold each lower edge.
B. Sepals: Inside reverse fold all edges.

8.
Mtn. fold edge behind to center of each petal & sepal.

9.
Turn model over. Proceed through Steps 10-16.

9.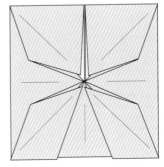

The Orchid

Top Half Only

17A.

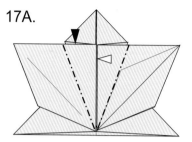

Inside reverse fold each petal.

17B.

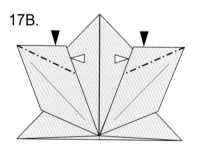

Inside reverse fold.

17C.

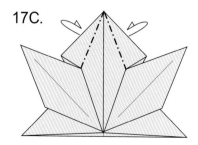

Mtn. fold behind.

The Orchid

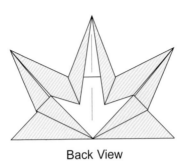

Back View

18.

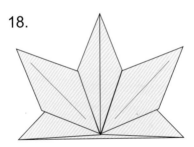

**Proceed from Step 19
to complete model.**

The Hula Dancer *(Mea Hula)*

The Hula Dancer *(Mea Hula)*

The Hula Dancer displays one side of the paper. Begin with the desired side down. Valley fold corner to corner; unfold. Repeat.

1.

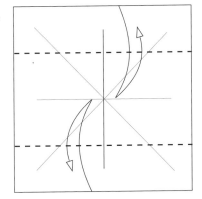

2.

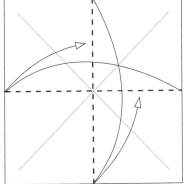

Valley fold edge to edge; unfold. Repeat.

3.

Valley fold edge to center; unfold. Repeat.

The Hula Dancer

4.

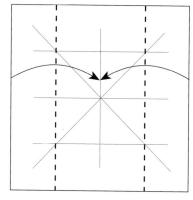

Valley fold edges to center.

5.

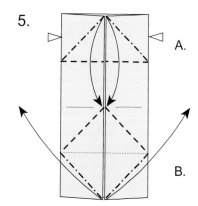

A. Fold points down.
B. Fold points up and out.

6.

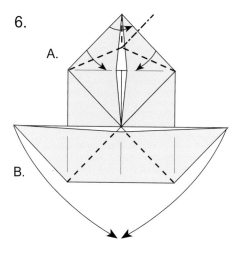

7.

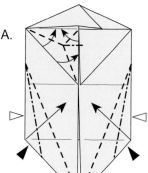

6.
A. Rabbit ear fold.
B. Valley fold flaps down.

7.
A. Rabbit ear fold.
B. Modified squash fold. See *The Humuhumu* (Steps 12a & 12b) for help.

8.
Valley fold arm up.

8.

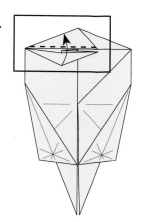

The Hula Dancer

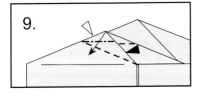

9.

Modified squash fold.

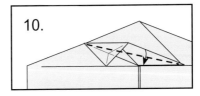

10.

Valley fold edge to edge;
unfold.

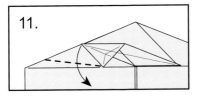

11.

Valley fold arm down on an angle.

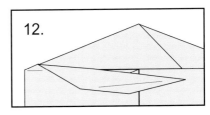

12.

Repeat Steps 7-11 on the right.

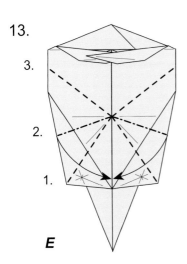

13.

3.

2.

1.

E

Fold in order shown:
1. Valley fold each edge in between center pt. & corner pt. of skirt.
2. Mtn. fold out from center line.
3. Flatten symmetrically. See 13a.

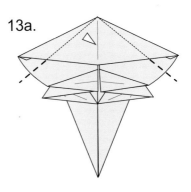

13a.

The Hula Dancer

14.

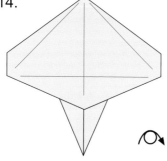

Turn model over.

15.

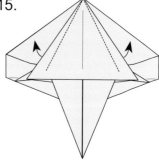

Refold skirt edges on
existing creases behind.

16.

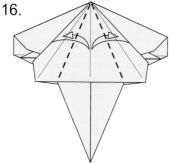

Valley fold skirt only;
unfold. Do not fold legs.

17.

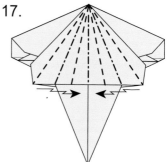

Mtn. fold skirt on existing
creases, then pleat.

18.

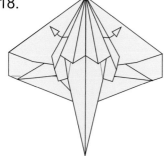

Unfold skirt on original edges.

19.

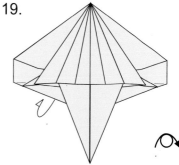

Mtn. fold head section
behind. **Turn model over.**

The Hula Dancer

20.

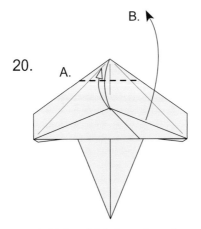

A. Valley fold pt. on top of
pt. of head; unfold.
B. Valley fold up.

21.

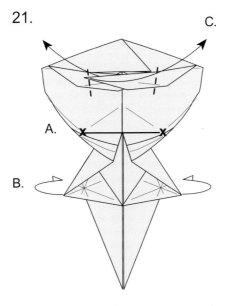

A. Pop out or refold pts. **x** outward.
B. Mtn. fold lower half together.
C. Fold arms back at widest
possible pt.

The Hula Dancer

22.

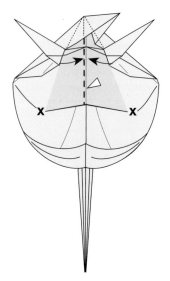

22a.

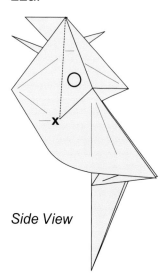

Side View

Push center line in to valley fold middle section (shaded area) in half. Note: Fold extends up to pt. of head. Top layer of head section is <u>not</u> folded in. Pinch length of folded section from behind to bring arms & pts. **x** tightly together. (22a)

23.

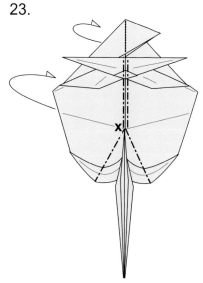

Starting from the top, pinch along folded section behind as you fold sides together.

The Hula Dancer

24.

A. Valley fold edge to edge; unfold.
B. Fold in order shown:
1. Valley fold edge along existing crease.
2. Pleat fold: Establish mtn. fold first.
Note: If folds do not intersect at pt. **x**, create new intersection pt.

Repeat 24B behind.

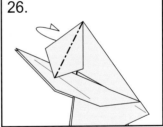

25.

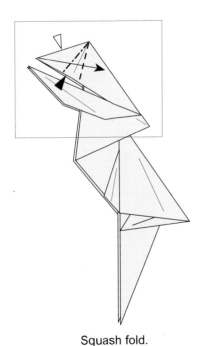

Squash fold.

26.

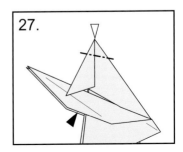

Mtn. fold in half.

27.

The Hula Dancer

Inside View of Result

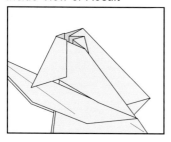

Open sink fold.

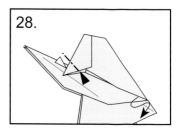

28.

A. Inside reverse fold.
B. Tuck corner under
   hair. Repeat behind.

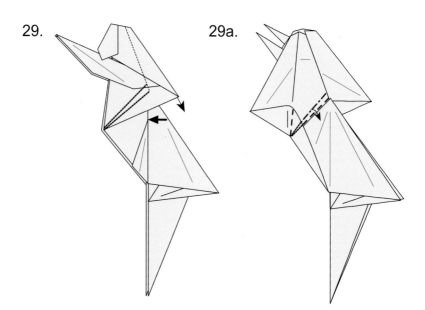

29.

29a.

Pleat fold inside section to tilt & lower top section to indicated pt:
1. Open back.
2. Valley fold along top edge of skirt. (29a)
3. Lower bodice to indicated pt. in Step 29.
4. Set mtn. fold.
5. Close sides.

The Hula Dancer

30.

31.

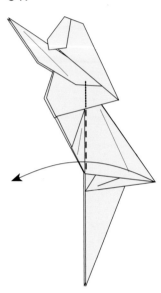

32.

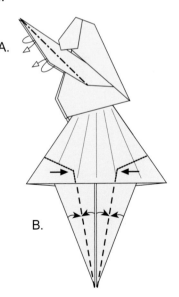

30.
Fold edges in 1/3 of
the distance to center.

31.
Valley fold side open.

32.
A. Refold on creases of
   Step 10. Unfold at a right
   angle.
B. Mtn. fold legs in half up
   to indicated pt.

A.

B.

The Hula Dancer

33.

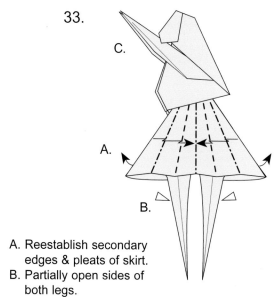

C.

A.

B.

A. Reestablish secondary
   edges & pleats of skirt.
B. Partially open sides of
   both legs.
C. Spread open arms.

See following
Optional Steps.

The Hula Dancer

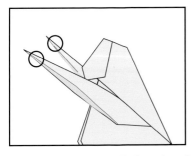 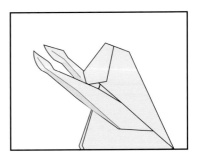

OPTIONAL: To form hands, pinch flat & bend slightly in.

The Double Hull Canoe
(Wa'a Kaulua)

The Double Hull Canoe *(Wa'a Kaulua)*

The Canoe displays one side of the paper. With the desired side down, begin with the Preliminary Fold.

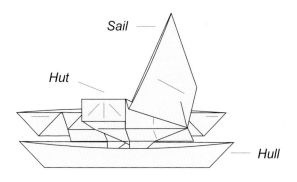

Sail

Hut

Hull

Model Description

1.

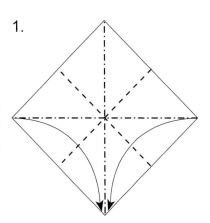

Note: First two folds are made on top layer only.

Fold: *a* to *b*.   Touch fold *c*.
     a to *c*.   Touch fold *d*.
     b to *d*.   Touch fold *e*.
     b to *e*.   Pre-crease *f*
              on **all** sections.
Unfold completely with desired side down.

2.

Proportioned Result

E

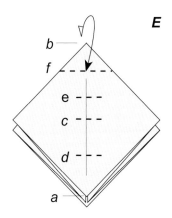

b
f
e
c
d
a

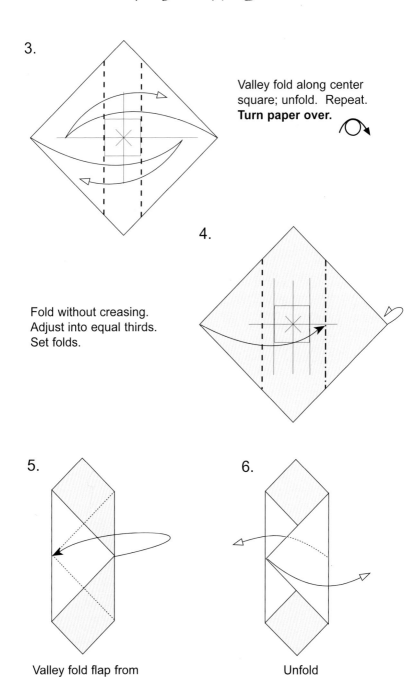

3.

Valley fold along center square; unfold. Repeat. **Turn paper over.**

4.

Fold without creasing. Adjust into equal thirds. Set folds.

5.

Valley fold flap from behind.

6.

Unfold

The Double Hull Canoe

7.

Valley fold on indicated crease intersections (equal thirds). **Unfold. Turn paper over.**

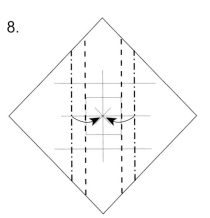

8.

8.
Pleat fold on existing creases.

9.
Valley fold edge to edge; unfold. Repeat.

10.
Valley fold section up on side of center square. Valley fold open sides on existing creases.

9.

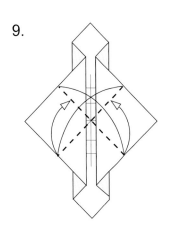

10.

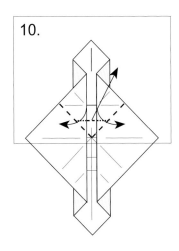

The Double Hull Canoe

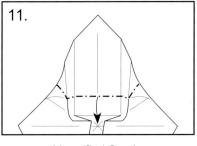

11.

Mtn. fold on existing creases to flatten section down. Repeat Steps 10 & 11 on lower half.

Magnified Section

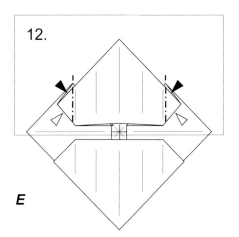

12.

E

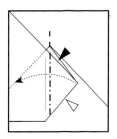

Inside reverse fold.

Note: Placement of fold to crease.

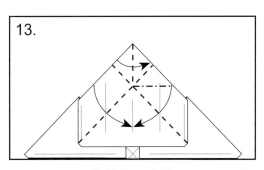

13.

Rabbit ear fold.

The Double Hull Canoe

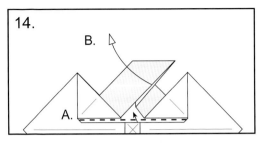

14.

A. Valley fold edge up; **unfold.**
B. Unfold rabbit ear fold.

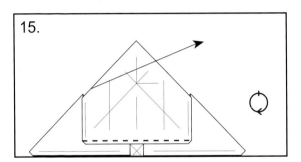

15.

Valley fold section perpendicular on
existing crease. **Rotate model.**

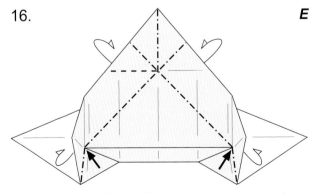

16. **E**

Pop out or refold indicated corner pts. outward
to mtn. fold edges under and to refold rabbit
ear fold. Maintain valley fold of Step 15.

The Double Hull Canoe

17.

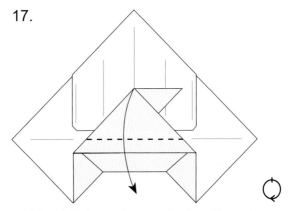

Valley fold down along center line. Repeat
Steps 13-17 on upper half. **Rotate model.**

18.
E

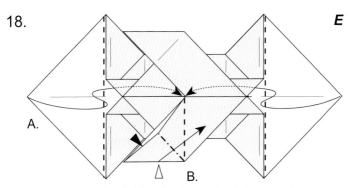

A.

B.

A. Valley fold both pts. under & in to center.
B. Squash fold flap.

19.

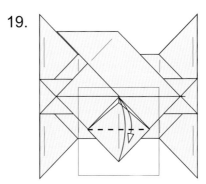

Valley fold pt. to pt.; unfold.

20.

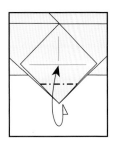

Pre-crease
all sections.

21.

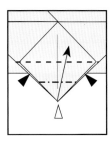

21a.

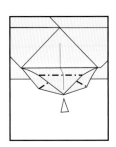

Flatten on pre-creases: 1.) Lift section.
2.) Open sides. 3.) Flatten. (21a)

22.

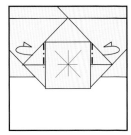

Mtn. fold tabs under.

23.

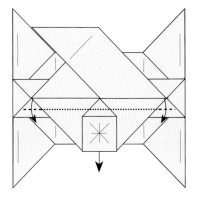

24.

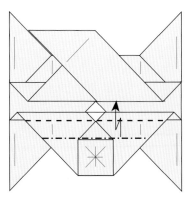

23.
Valley fold section down
at furthest possible pt.

24.
Pleat fold: Establish mtn.
fold first along edge of hut.

The Double Hull Canoe

25.

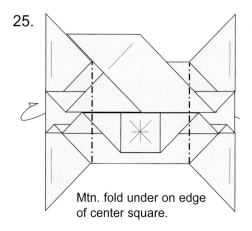

Mtn. fold under on edge
of center square.

26.

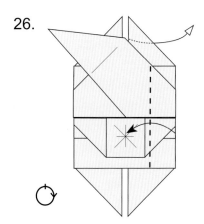

26.
Valley fold edge only to
center. **Rotate model.**

27.
Valley fold edge to
edge.

27.

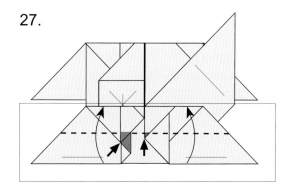

The Double Hull Canoe

28.   *Magnified Section*

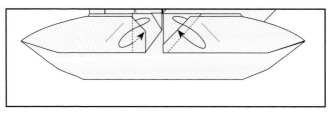

Tuck edge beneath layer below. Note: Shaded sections
indicated in Step 27 are reverse folded in.

29.

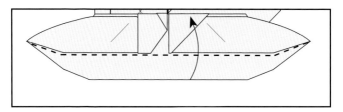

Valley fold side of hull up. Repeat
Steps 26-29 on other side.

30.

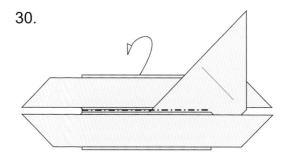

Mtn. fold in half.

31.

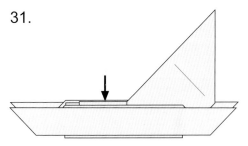

Hold center pleat. Unfold all other
sections at right angles.

32.

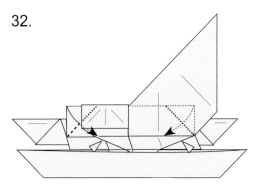

Lift layers to valley fold corners
beneath hut & sail down.

33.

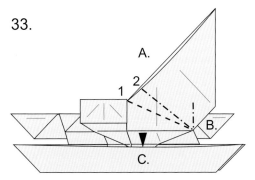

A. Pleat fold. Valley fold then mtn. fold.
   Unfold both folds at a right angle.
B. Mtn. fold sail at base.
C. Partially open hulls.

The Double Hull Canoe

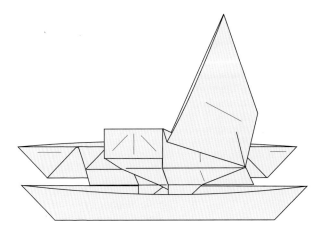

The Bird of Paradise

The Bird of Paradise displays both sides of the paper. The flower bract, stem, and corolla exhibit one side; the sepals exhibit the other. Select paper with contrasting sides.

Select paper at least 10 inches square.

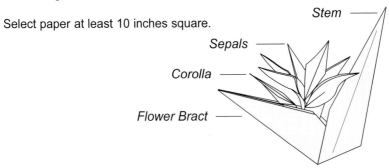

Model Description

With the color of the sepals up, begin with the Preliminary Fold.

Squash fold each flap.

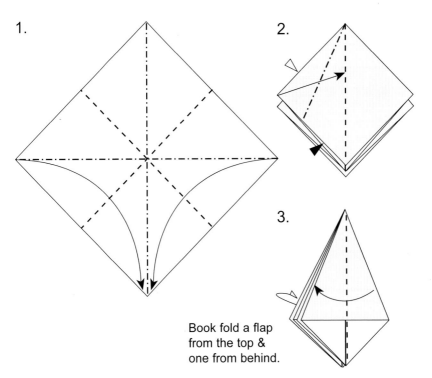

1.

2.

3.

Book fold a flap from the top & one from behind.

The Bird of Paradise

4.

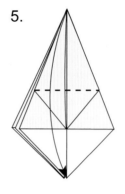

Petal fold.

5.

Valley fold flap down.

6.

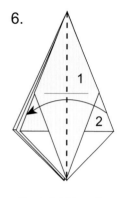

Book fold two flaps.

7.

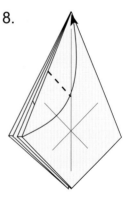

E

Valley fold pt. to
corner; unfold. Repeat.

8.

Valley fold corner
to pt.

9.

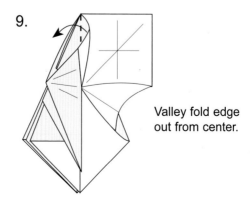

Valley fold edge
out from center.

The Bird of Paradise

10.

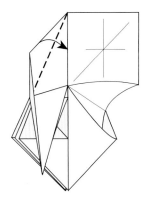

10.
Valley fold edge
to center.

11.
Fold crease to
center.

11.

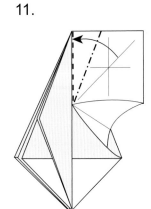

12.

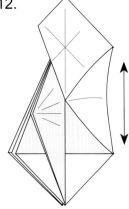

12.
Stretch mid-section.
Form precise pts.
Flatten symmetrically.

13.
Book fold two flaps
from behind. **Turn
model over.**

13.

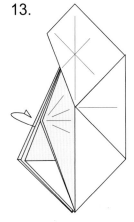

14.

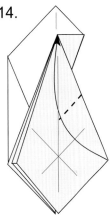

14.
Repeat Step 7, then
Step 10 (shown) to
Step 13 on the right.

15.
Fold edge behind to
center. **Rotate model.**

15.

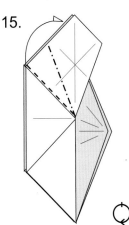

16. Petal fold.

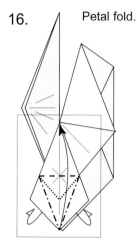

17.

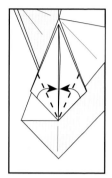

Valley fold edges to center. **Unfold petal fold completely.**

18.

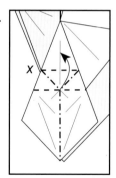

Note: All creases but *x* are existing through Step 20. Reestablish mtn. folds. Valley fold up on *x*. Valley fold sides in.

19.

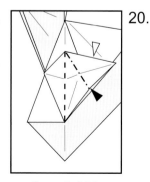

Squash fold.

20.

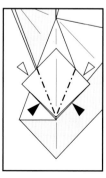

Inside reverse fold both sides.

21.

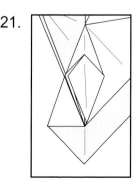

Repeat Steps 15-20 behind.

The Bird of Paradise

22.

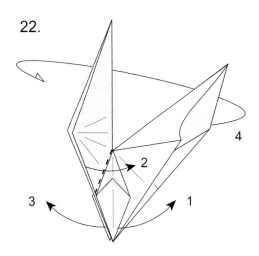

Fold in order shown:
1. Pull section out & up.
2. Valley fold side open.
3. Pull section behind out & up.
4. Mtn. fold side open.

Flatten to set folds.

23.

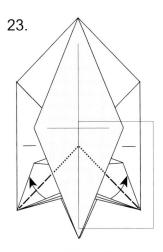

Book fold two flaps
up on each side.

24.

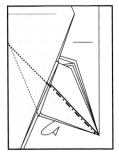

Mtn. fold both layers
into first pocket behind.
Maintain valley fold of
Step 22. Re-flatten
sides open.

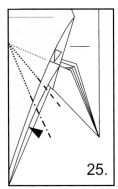

25.

Inside reverse fold
inner layer.

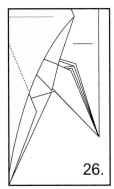

26.

Repeat Steps 24
& 25 on the left.

27.

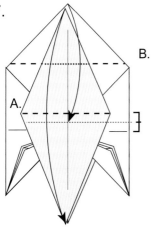

B.

A.

A. Valley fold flap in half.
B. Valley fold pt. down
   between folded edge
   of flap & crease.

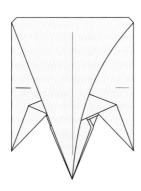

Result
Note: Right side shows
inside view. Current fold
matches reverse fold of
Step 26.

28.

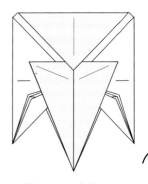

Turn model over.

29.

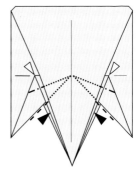

Inside reverse fold
inside layers.

30.

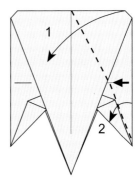

1

2

Valley fold in order. Existing
crease establishes indicated
pt. Smooth excess paper to
indicated pt.

The Bird of Paradise

31.

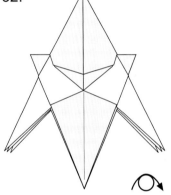

A. Tuck excess paper under top layer.
B. Valley fold edge to edge.

Repeat Steps 30 & 31 on the left.

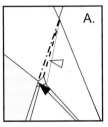

Magnified Section

E

32.

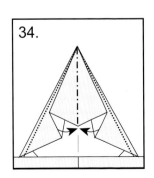

Turn model over.

33.

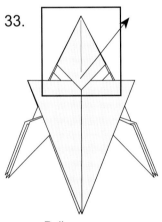

Pull up
trapped paper.

34.

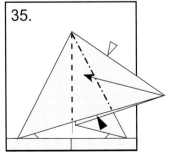

Wrap tightly around
edges. Fold flap in half.

35.

Squash fold.

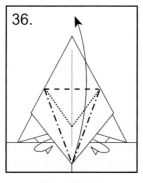

36.

Petal Fold.

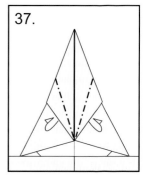

37.

Mtn. fold edge
behind to center.

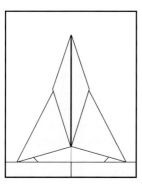

Result

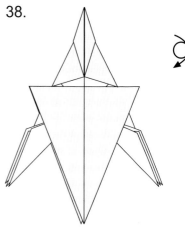

38.

Turn model over.

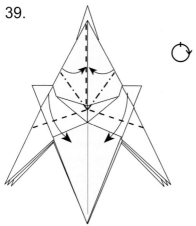

39.

Rabbit ear fold. Match
edges of bracts beneath.
Rotate model.

The Bird of Paradise

40.

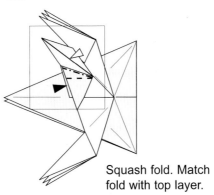

Squash fold. Match
fold with top layer.

41.

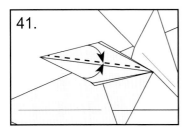

Valley fold layers up.

42.

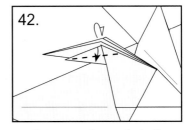

Fold outer layers in half.

43.

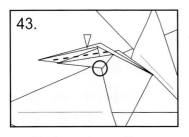

Pinch as shown. Flatten
layers open at center.

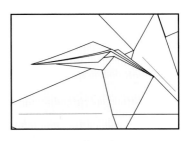

Result

The Bird of Paradise

44.

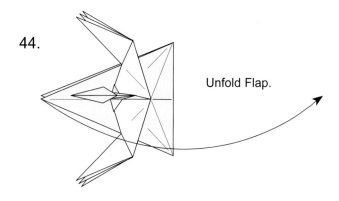

Unfold Flap.

45.

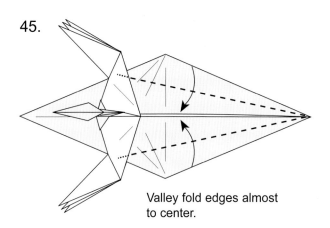

Valley fold edges almost to center.

46.

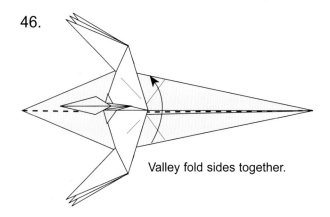

Valley fold sides together.

47.

MODEL STYLE 1
with Stem

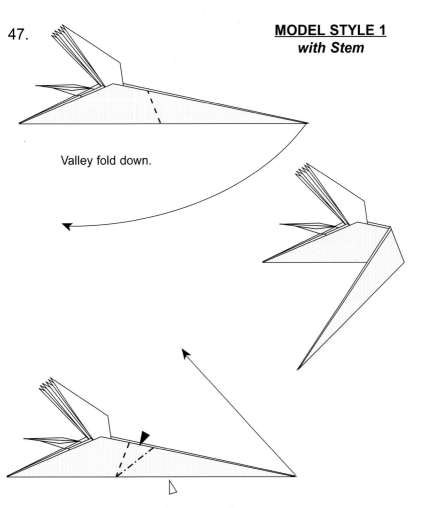

Valley fold down.

Squash fold at an offset.

MODEL STYLE 2
with Leaf Tip

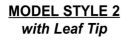

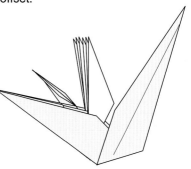

The Bird of Paradise

Use the following steps as a guide to opening & arranging the sepals.

48.

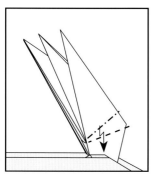

Pleat fold outer sepals.

49.

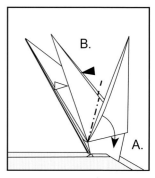

A. Open between layers
of sepal color.
B. Inside reverse fold.

50.

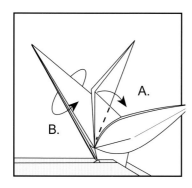

A. Valley fold sides open.
B. Curl sepal.

51.

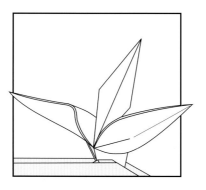

Repeat on selected sepals
behind.

Shape sepals and corolla
as desired.

The Bird of Paradise

The Torch Ginger
('Awapuhi ko'oko'o))

The Torch Ginger *('Awapuhi koʻokoʻo)*

The Torch Ginger displays one side of the paper. Spot layering instructions follow.

Select paper at least 10 inches square.

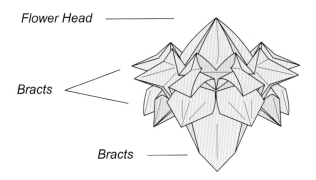

Flower Head ——————

Bracts <

Bracts ——————

With the desired side down, begin with the Preliminary Fold.

Model Description

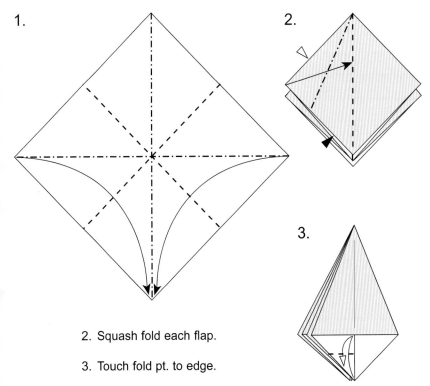

1.

2.

3.

2. Squash fold each flap.

3. Touch fold pt. to edge.

The Torch Ginger

4.

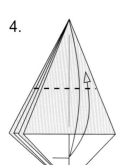

Valley fold pt. to
crease; unfold.

5.

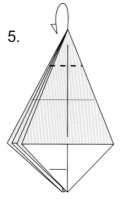

Mtn. fold pt. behind
to crease.

6.

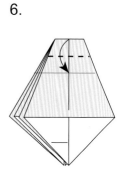

Valley fold edge
only to crease.

7.

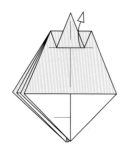

8.

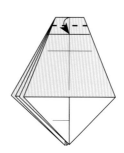

9.

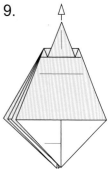

10.

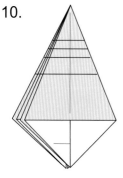

7. Unfold last fold.

8. Valley fold edge only to crease.

9. Unfold.

10. Pre-crease all folds on **all** sections.
Unfold completely with desired side up.

11.

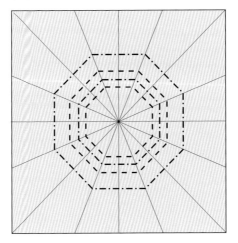

Define creases if necessary.

Important: All folds must be accurate.
Rings of creases are concentric.

12.

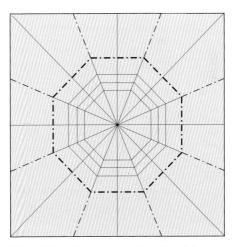

Mtn. fold edges down. Reestablish
diagonals to produce accurate pts.

13.

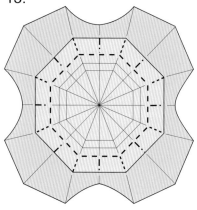

Valley fold new edge up. Refold model to produce pts. & to check accuracy of folds.

Note: Valley folds are mtn. folds & vice versa within outer rings.

14.

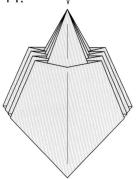

Side View
Note: All flaps are identical. Model lays flat. Adjust folds if necessary.

Partially unfold model. Flatten pt. & center section.

15.

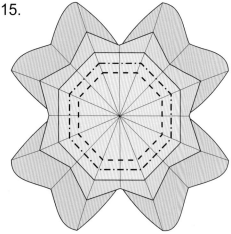

Mtn. fold & valley fold to create a new edge.

The Torch Ginger

16.

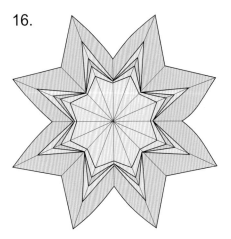

Refold model.
Note: Valley folds are
mtn. folds & vice versa
within last 2 rings.

17.

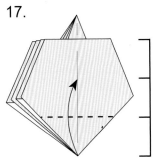

Valley fold pt. up to 1/3 distance
from top edge. Repeat on
remaining 3 sections. **Unfold.**

18.

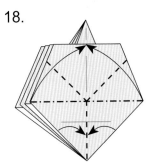

Rabbit ear fold. Valley
fold corner pt. up to
center of edge.

19.

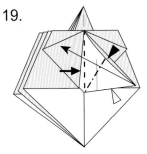

Note: Indicated edge does not lie
on center line.

Squash fold flap. Repeat Steps 18
& 19 on remaining 3 sections.

20.   *E*

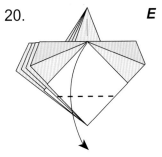

Valley fold pt. down
on crease of Step 17.

21.

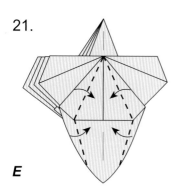

E

Valley fold edges in.

22.

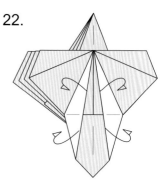

Mtn. fold edges behind.
Partially unfold to accomplish.
(22a) Repeat Steps 20-22 on 3
remaining sections.

22a.

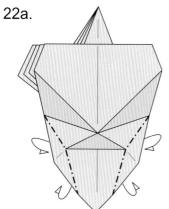

23.

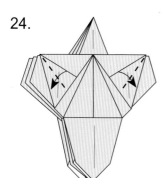

Inside reverse fold
at an offset. (To
begin, mtn. fold
edge to center.)

24.

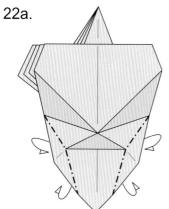

Reverse fold edge out.
Repeat Steps 23 & 24
on remaining sections.

25.

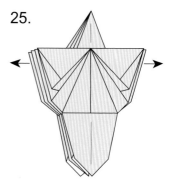

Expand model.

The Torch Ginger

26.

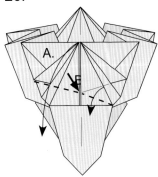

A. Valley fold each bract down to find indicated pt. Unfold.
B. Valley fold edge of topmost layer down. Do not flatten.

27.

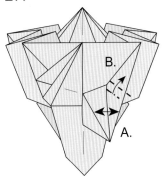

A. Stretch apart overlap on top of bract only.
B. Pleat fold to create outer edge. Flatten bract.

Repeat Steps 26B & 27 on left bract.
Repeat Steps 26 & 27 on remaining sections.

28.

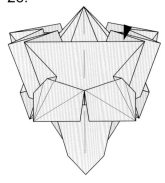

Open sides to expose inside fold.

29.

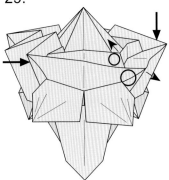

A. Pinch corners. Pull apart to raise & extend edge.
B. Repeat Steps 28 & 29 on indicated adjacent flaps.

The Torch Ginger

30.

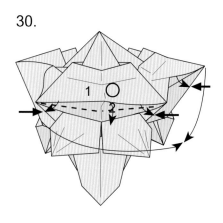

1. Pinch layers together up to crease of ridge. Valley fold lower edges of midsection down.
2. Compress pertaining flaps completely together to accomplish & set folds. Release. Note: When flaps are compressed completely, edges of midsection should align with indicated edges.

Repeat Steps 28, 29A, & 30 on each remaining flap.

Fold mid-pt. of each edge down. Compress flaps together to set each fold. Release.

31.

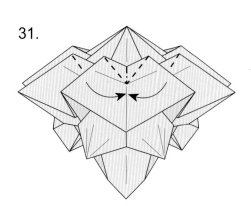

32.

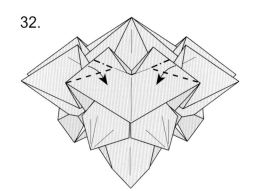

Fold side edges of each midsection in.

33.

Fold sections of lower
edge of midsection
to center.

34.

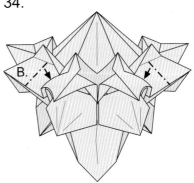

A. Repeat Step 33 on
   remaining sections.
B. Pinch close pertaining
   section without bracts; then
   mtn. fold to define noted
   edges of all similar bracts.

35.

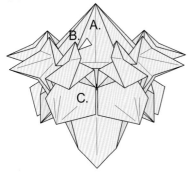

A. Insert a stick or a pencil through
   bottom hole of model. On alternating
   sections of the flower head, push center
   crease (A) outward to round section.
   Keep sections without bracts closed.
B. Round out edges of all top bracts.
C. Lift & round all lower bracts.

OPTIONAL STEM: Insert a paper-covered or painted dowel of an
appropriate size through the bottom hole of the model.

The Torch Ginger

Spot Layering Instructions

Read the section on *Layering*.

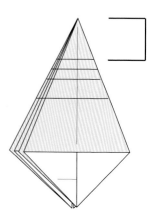

To spot layer paper for *The Torch Ginger*, complete Steps 1-10 of the general instructions. Although you need only to determine the crease of Step 5, it is best to establish all creases before spot layering. Measure the exact distance from the tip to the crease of Step 5. Multiply the distance by two to arrive at the number of square inches of the spot layer. For example: the distance would measure 1.5 inches on a model folded from a 10-inch square. Therefore, the spot layer would be a 3-inch square.

To fold your spot layer, begin with the desired side down. Complete Steps 1 & 2 of the general instructions for The Torch Ginger.

1.   **2.**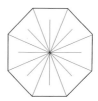

The Torch Ginger

1. Cut off lower sections to create an octagon.
2. Unfold spot layer.
3. Unfold model completely with desired side up.
4. Spray back of spot layer with adhesive.
5. Align center pt., valley & mtn. folds. Adhere spot layer to base layer.
6. Refold. Reestablish crease of Step 5 on all sections. Continue with general instructions.

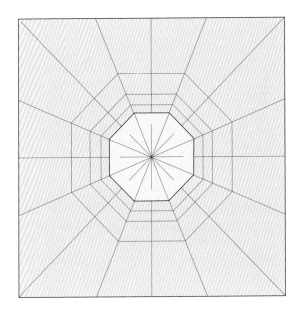

From a Sea of Paper

In this section you will learn how to incorporate many different types of paper into the art of origami and how to create models similar to those in this book. You will learn a simple way to cut a perfectly square sheet of paper, and a method for designing custom paper. In the *Layering* and *Wet Folding* sections, you will also learn how to utilize types of paper that are otherwise impossible to fold, and find tips on using printed paper and on selecting paper. This section begins with information on origami paper, which is indispensable if you prefer not to cut your own paper.

Note: Some of the methods in this section may appear a little extensive for origami. You will find that the methods, once applied, are actually simple, and that the results are well worth the time and effort. You will also find that the precautionary steps are important, especially when working with paper you value.

Origami Paper

Origami paper is suitably thin paper that is perfectly square*. It is a distinct form of paper that generally folds easily, producing crisp and well-defined models. Origami paper typically offers color on one side (the other is usually white). It is available in an assortment of solid colors, patterns, and prints. Origami paper ranges in size from approximately 2 to 14-inches square. However, you will find nearly all patterns and prints are sold only in 6-inch squares. You may purchase origami paper at art, craft, and hobby supply stores or at stores that specialize in Japanese merchandise. Origami paper (6 and 10-inches square or larger in assorted colors) is suggested for the projects of this book.

*Rarely, you may find packets of origami paper that are not perfectly square. The discrepancies are usually slight and generally consistent throughout a packet. If you plan to trim your paper, please read *Definition of a Perfect Square* first.

Cutting the Perfect Square

Benefits. You will benefit from an incredible selection and supply of suitable paper if you decide to cut your own paper for origami. Your selection will consist of an array of specialty and decorative paper from around the world, including gift wrap, packaging, stationery, and paper used for drawing, painting, and printmaking. It will also extend to include paper napkins, newspapers, and magazines. By cutting your own paper, you will also be able to produce squares large enough to create models of notable size. Beginning with a large square will also facilitate folding the more complex models. Above all, you will be able to create beautiful and unique models.

Definition of a Perfect Square. A square is defined as having four sides equal in length and four equal angles of 90 degrees. It is important in origami that all the conditions of a square are met. Any variance, however slight, will produce an imperfect square which can make folding difficult and may also result in an obvious distortion of your model.

Templates. The easiest way to cut a perfect square is to use a template. A template can be easily positioned anywhere on your paper. Held securely in place, it can be traced with an X-acto knife on a cutting mat, quickly producing a square sheet OR it can be lightly traced with a pencil. The square can then be cut out with a pair of sharp scissors. Perfectly square templates can be found on the Internet at web sites that sell origami supplies. These templates range in even-numbered sizes from 4 to 12-inches square and include 3, 5, 18, and 24-inch squares. They are made from hard plastic and are guaranteed to be perfectly square.

Quilting Squares. Quilting squares make ideal templates and are highly recommended for origami. Quality quilting squares are made from clear acrylic and are perfectly square within .002 inch accuracy. The templates have precise grid measurements which allow you to accurately create smaller squares of all sizes. In addition, grid measurements are marked in both yellow and black, which are easily seen on either dark or light paper. Quilting squares can be found in quilting specialty shops, sewing centers and craft stores. They are available in 4, 6, 9-1/2, 12-1/2 and 15-inch squares. Select the larger sizes if possible.

Alternative Templates. You can have templates made at plastic shops that manufacture acrylic products. Specify that your template must be a perfect square and ask for a guarantee. Be sure that all edges are smooth and flawless before accepting your template. You can also create a perfectly square template from a pair of identical right angles (available in even-numbered sizes between 4 and 12-inches at art supply stores). Select clear, non-tinted, acrylic angles. Avoid angles with beveled edges. Before purchasing, form a square. The tips of the angles should match precisely on both ends. Your square should also be a uniform thickness and all edges should be flawless. To join the angles together, align the angles sides precisely and tape on one side of the template only with strong (preferably clear) tape. Fold your template in half to store.

Other Tools. An X-acto knife and a cutting mat are very practical and highly recommended. You can produce a cut square cleanly, quickly, and without marking your paper. Choose No. 11 blades for your X-acto knife to produce the appropriate cut. A cutting mat offers a safe, non-slip surface that reseals itself after each cut. Select a size that will easily accommodate a large template. Purchase X-acto knives and cutting mats at art, craft, and hobby stores. You can also find cutting mats at sewing centers.

Selecting Paper

When selecting paper, feel it to judge its thickness and malleability before purchasing. Also feel the combined thickness of several sheets to determine the resulting thickness of a model's folded layers. Be aware that paper may vary within a specific type. It may differ between manufacturers and whether it is hand or machine made. Handmade paper may differ greatly from sheet to sheet. Examine each sheet if possible. When ordering by mail, it is recommended that you obtain or purchase a book of swatches.

Printed Paper

It is almost impossible to foresee the result of a model folded from paper printed with large designs. For this reason, it is suggested that you create a *blueprint* before cutting your paper. A blueprint is created by folding a model of the intended size from tracing paper. The parts of the model are outlined and labeled. The model is then completely unfolded, revealing the layout of its parts. Without a blueprint, your model may not properly display the design of your print. Desired portions may be excluded or upside down. Use your blueprint to help position your template to achieve the desired results.

Layering

Definition and Applications. Layering is a process by which you create a special sheet of paper for a particular model by adhering selected sheets of paper together. The selected sheets are chosen for their color, texture, malleability, and/or strength, with regard to thickness. Layers are arranged and combined with a spray adhesive, enabling you to determine the color and texture of each side. In this manner, you can design paper for models exhibiting both sides of the paper, such as *The Bird of Paradise*. You can also create your own colors by fusing together colors of various types of paper. The process of layering permits you to utilize materials such as aluminum foil and types of paper that are too thin, soft, or difficult to fold. Foil-based paper allows you to mold your model into otherwise unobtainable dimensional forms. An example is *The Hibiscus*. By **Spot Layering**, a modified form of layering, you can create a specific color pattern, as seen in *The Torch Ginger*. Color patterns can also be created by positioning and layering printed paper, as seen in *The Orchid*. You can use both types of layering to strengthen your paper to hold a form and/or prevent it from tearing. Layering allows you to achieve degrees of realism and to create beautiful models.

Base Layers and Overlays. Sheets of paper used in layering are referred to as either the *base layer* or the *overlay*. The base layer, or foundation, is typically the thickest of the sheets of paper you plan to combine. The base layer determines the strength of your layered paper and the dimensional form of your model. It supplies color to transparent overlays such as cellophane and depth of color to translucent overlays such as tissue or rice paper. The overlay is generally a type of paper that is unsuitable for folding. Overlays may be applied to both sides of the base layer and/or added in layers on either side. The overlay, if not transparent, provides the different sides of your paper with its initial color or with complete color. It also provides surface texture.

Selecting Paper and Adhesives. Examples of paper created by layering are seen in many of the presentation models included in this book. Descriptions accompany each model, and paper combinations are listed for all layered paper. When selecting paper for layering, refer to the various models and their descriptions for layering formulas and ideas.

The resulting thickness of your paper is an important factor when selecting paper. Generally, the thickness of each selected sheet should be equivalent to the thickness of no more than one or two sheets of newspaper. As a rule, if more than two sheets of paper are to be combined, all overlays should be about as thin as tissue paper. Also remember to take into account that the spray adhesive will contribute to the thickness of the layered paper. This added thickness can make a difference, especially if several layers are adhered together. Ideally, your spray adhesive should be thin, but still bond well. Choose an adhesive that will also allow you to reposition your overlays if needed. Spray adhesives are available at art, craft, and hobby stores. Ask the salesperson to recommend the thinnest spray or test the fluidity and thickness of each spray by shaking the can. Avoid *low mist* sprays as they tend to fall heavily upon your paper. Read the labels.

Samples. The added thickness of your spray adhesive makes it hard to determine the actual thickness of your layered paper without first adhering the sheets together. The resulting color of the combined layers is also difficult to foresee until the layers are fused, but stacking sheets of uncut paper in order can provide you with a general idea of thickness and color. If you are at all uncertain about the outcome of your selections, make a sample, particularly if your paper is expensive, in limited supply, or if you are layering paper of very large dimensions. Use a scrap piece or take a sample from a section you will not be using. Make your sample large enough so that you can fold it over repeatedly, enabling you to judge the combined thickness of folded layers. Test to see how your paper pre-creases as well as creases. Test for strength and malleability. Label and keep your sample for future reference.

Paper Suggestions. Generally, certain types of paper are used as base layers and other types as overlays.

Base Layers

Although many forms of thin paper make suitable base layers, only the different types of foil are mentioned. Foil has the most to offer as a base layer. It adds dimension and stability to form, and the fusion of its reflective color with very thin sheets of overlay is unmatched.

<u>Origami Foil.</u> Highly recommended. Thinner than foil gift wrap. Available in several beautiful colors and backed with white paper. Sold in packets up to 10-inches square and in large sheets (15" x 18").

<u>Foil Gift Wrap.</u> Paper backed. Inexpensive. Can provide a base layer up to 30-inches square.

<u>Aluminum Foil.</u> Provides an extremely malleable base. Very difficult to fold.

<u>Florist Foil.</u> Similar to light-duty aluminum foil. Mainly available with color on one side only. Sold in many colors on rolls or by requested lengths at flower and garden shops or craft stores.

Overlays

Only a few types are noted. Basically any type of paper or fabric is suitable as long as it is thin-to-very thin.

<u>Tissue Paper.</u> Ideally very thin and translucent. Available in many colors. Printed and metallic tissue are usually slightly thicker and not as porous.

From a Sea of Paper

Cellophane.* Available in tints and various colors. Provides a glossy texture.

Crepe Paper. Textured. Stretchable. Not colorfast.

Unryu. Varies in thickness and texture. Contains decorative threads or fibers.

Lace Paper.* Available in several beautiful patterns. Light and airy with a soft texture.

Silky Tissue. Very thin and strong.

Fantasy Paper. Lightweight tissue. Contains real leaves, ferns, butterfly wings, etc.

Chiri. Translucent. Available in assorted colors. Contains flecks of bark.

Mango or Banana Paper. Contains flecks of mango or banana leaves.

Sanwa Tissue. Extremely thin with swirls of fiber. May contain flecks of silver and gold.

Fashion Paper. Sold in sheets or as packets of napkins. Very strong and available in many prints and colors. Napkins are very thin.

*See How to Layer for special instructions.

How To Layer:

- Choose a sheltered but well-ventilated area to apply your spray adhesive.
- Protect the surface to be used with a sheet of paper. Do not use newspaper as the ink may smudge your paper. Use the walls of a large cardboard box to contain the overspray.
- A paper-covered board on which to place and carry your paper is recommended. You may not wish to work or linger in the area where your adhesive is sprayed. Paper that has just been sprayed is difficult to handle and is easily transported on a board.
- Cut your base layer into a perfect square of the desired dimension. Roughly cut your overlay larger than your base layer, even if it is placed off-center. Your overlay should be large enough so that it will still cover your base layer. In the event your overlay is a square of the desired size, roughly cut your base layer larger.

From a Sea of Paper

- Secure your paper to the covered board or surface. The force of the spray can lift the corners of the paper and you may accidentally spray the back of the your paper (or the paper may roll onto itself). To secure the paper, lightly spray (see following step) the covered board or surface with adhesive and let dry. The dried spray should provide enough tack to hold the paper down. It is not necessary to continuously change the protective covering of your board or surface. Be aware that the accumulated spray will eventually lift off. It will show on dark or reflective surfaces. Initially, you can also use very small pieces of double-stick tape. Handle the pieces of tape until they are tacky rather than sticky, so that they do not tear your paper.
- Follow the directions on the can of adhesive. Wear a mask and safety glasses. Make note of the drying time.
- Spray the adhesive onto your base layer. Be sure to spray all edges. Spray your overlay only if it is of the desired size or if it is to be *spot layered.*
- Spray a *light* coat of adhesive on your base layer to adhere very thin and porous overlays such as tissue paper. Too much adhesive spray may ripple the overlay.
- Lightly spray the edges of <u>cellophane</u> (or other non-textured, slippery overlays) in addition to spraying the entire base layer to ensure that the edges do not separate.
- After spraying the adhesive, place your base layer on a clean, flat surface. Apply your overlay before the noted drying time. Always apply your overlay to the base layer, not the other way around.
- When adhering layers together, especially those of large dimensions, hold the overlay over the base layer and align on a lower corner. Slowly smooth the overlay down, working diagonally. A roller is very useful to press and seal the layers together.
- When all overlays have been adhered, trim along the edges of the base layer with a straight edge and an X-acto knife or cut with a sharp pair of scissors.
- <u>Spot Layering.</u> Fold the base layer to determine the position and dimensions of the overlay. Follow the instructional procedure of the model until a crease outline of the pattern of the overlay is established. Measure and cut the overlay paper to fit within the crease outline.
- Always spray the overlay to be spot layered, not the base layer.
- <u>Lace</u> and other airy types of paper will stick to protective paper coverings. Use wax paper or plastic instead. Spray the overlay, immediately peel it from the sheet, and position it on the base layer.

Wet Folding

Definition. Wet folding is a process which enables you to fold thicker paper and/or types of paper that normally crack when creased. In wet folding, paper is carefully dampened to make it malleable enough to fold. A wet-folded model will often hold its form when it dries. Therefore, wet folding can provide your model with sculpted effect.

Samples. To determine if your paper will withstand wet folding and how much moisture to apply, it is recommended that you work with a sample. Use a scrap piece or take your sample from a section of uncut paper you won't be using. Slowly dampen your sample until it is malleable enough to fold. You can determine the strength of your wet paper by folding and unfolding the sample repeatedly. <u>Optional:</u> Continue to dampen a separate portion of your sample to determine at what point the paper will weaken and tear. This will reveal how much leeway you have when dampening and folding your paper.

Methods. Before you dampen your paper, take into consideration the dimension and thickness of the paper and how much moisture needs to be applied. Based on your assessment, use either a damp cloth, paper towel, sponge, mist bottle, or even your wet hands. Systematically and evenly dampen the back of the paper until it is malleable, as determined by your sample. If your paper becomes too wet, leave it to dry. During the course of folding, you may have to re-dampen your model or portions of it. Select a more suitable dampening method if necessary.

You may also slowly and evenly dampen you paper by applying a single layer of damp paper towels to the back of your paper and/or sample and regulating the dampness of the paper towels. Press the paper towels against the entire surface area of your paper and/or sample. Cover with a sheet of plastic (an unused garbage bag works fine). Place an object of evenly-distributed weight on top (you can use your cutting mat, a board, magazines, or books). Check the paper periodically by folding your sample to test its malleability.

Paper Description of Models

Aloha Shirts

Red and Yellow Prints: Fabric layered on silver foil gift wrap.

Center Model: Island Heritage gift wrap.

Volcano

Crater: Thai reversible unryu.

Eruption: Thai unryu layered on gold foil gift wrap.

Humuhumunukunukuāpuaʻa

Thai Batik hand-made and hand-painted paper.

Anthurium

Tissue paper layered on both sides of florist foil. Cellophane layered onto side representing the bract.

Hibiscus

Crepe paper layered onto both sides of aluminum foil.

Plumeria

Origami paper.

White Plumeria: Origami paper spot-layered with yellow tissue.

Marlin

Mulberry tissue layered onto both sides of origami foil paper.

Geckos
Origami paper.

Snow King Protea
Hand-made paper spot-layered with Thai soft unryu.

Orchids
Printed tissue positioned, then layered onto both sides of origami foil paper.
Large Orchid: Hand-made tissue layered onto origami foil and aluminum foil.

Hula Dancers
Crumpled tissue layered onto mulberry paper. (Skirt of model was partially unfolded, then stamped with Hawaiian quilt pattern.)

Double Hull Canoe
Tapa. (Model was folded, then hand-painted.)

Bird of Paradise
Green and blue Japanese tissue positioned and layered onto florist foil. Tissue paper (orange) layered onto the other (back) side.
Giant Bird of Paradise: Green and blue Japanese tissue positioned and layered onto florist foil. Silky tissue layered onto the other (back) side.

Torch Ginger
Fabric (taffeta) layered onto silver gift wrap, then spot-layered with Japanese lace.